18.99

Learning Centre

Hayes Community Campus

Coldharbour Lane, Hayes, Middx, UB3 3BB

Renewals: 01895 85 3740

FU LEARNING

INVOLVE ME AND I'LL UNDERSTAND

Please return this item to the Learning Centre on or before the last date stamped below:

370.15

FULL ON
LEARNING

INVOLVE ME AND I'LL UNDERSTAND

ZOË ELDER
EDITED BY IAN GILBERT

Crown House Publishing Limited
www.crownhouse.co.uk
www.crownhousepublishing.com

First published by
Crown House Publishing Ltd
Crown Buildings, Bancyfelin, Carmarthen, Wales, SA33 5ND, UK
www.crownhouse.co.uk

and

Crown House Publishing Company LLC
6 Trowbridge Drive, Suite 5, Bethel, CT 06801, USA
www.crownhousepublishing.com

British Library of Cataloguing-in-Publication Data
A catalogue entry for this book is available from the British Library.

Print ISBN: 978-184590681-8
ePub ISBN: 978-184590839-3
Mobi ISBN: 978-184590838-6

LCCN 2010937326

Printed and bound by
Oriental Press, Dubai

To Lucy, Mum, Dad and Nev

ACKNOWLEDGEMENTS

This book is a (deep) breath in between the thousands of conversations about learning I have enjoyed during my career. Being aware of how much just one person can influence the thinking of another means that it is impossible for me to thank the many voices that resonate in this book. But rest assured, you're all in here. All of you. Thank you.

For over fifteen years, I have been fortunate to learn alongside pupils, teachers, advisers and schools around the country. Every shard of insight, challenge and reflection they have gifted me has inspired and shaped my thoughts to this point in time. I know that more will follow tomorrow and I thank you for these.

Producing a book like this requires every one of the dispositions we seek to draw out in every one of our learners; collaboration and discernment, questioning, curiosity, reflection, passion, resilience and creativity, to name a few. I have experienced just such a collection of dispositions in the unfailing support and encouragement of both Ian Gilbert, the founder of Independent Thinking and Caroline Lenton at Crown House Publishing. They enabled me to find the courage to put down on paper what has been in my head for so long. Thanks also to Tom Fitton, who has skilfully brought the design ideas in this book to life. You've been brilliant, 'Team Full On'.

It was suggested in the early stages of writing this book that I may have 'used all the words up', so a long time ago, early one very cold Sunday morning, I squirrelled a small handful of words safely away for one really important voice (who also, fittingly, gets the last word) …

Thank you, Lucy.

FOREWORD

'Oooh look! A bandwagon. Come on everybody ...!'

I'm paraphrasing (a bit) but this sums up a great deal of in-service teacher training that takes place not only in the UK but also around the world. On one hand, it proves that good teachers are, despite being very busy people, always on the lookout for ways of being better at what they do. Let's not knock that. Teachers always seem to be on the receiving end of the blame for society's ills yet most are hard working, committed people who are genuinely trying to do the right thing for the young people in their care. In the UK, if a child isn't learning the teacher at least shoulders some of the responsibility and tries to do something about it. This may sound obvious in these days of accountability and progress but it has not always been the case and it certainly isn't always so elsewhere in the world. 'Get yourself a tutor' seems to be the main response from teachers in my part of the world currently, 'It's not my fault they didn't learn what I taught them.'

And with such a sense of accountability comes a preparedness to countenance new ideas if they think it will help.

The downside is that this drive to be better, when it is matched with the incessant busy-ness of school life, means teachers often tend to be on the lookout for a quick fix. A silver bullet. A magic pill they can pick up and hand out to all on the way into the lesson for instant results. All of which means we leap on the next snake oil-selling, pill-toting, bullet-vending fixer that comes our way marketing some new 'system' that will answer our floor target prayers.

But what happens when, after a lesson spent drinking water, doing Brain Gym, using Prezi and only learning if the teaching matches our 'preferred learning modality' ('I'm a kinesthetic learner so can I mime the answers to this worksheet, Miss?'), you suddenly realise that the same old children who weren't learning before aren't learning now?

Of course, the flip side of easy-to-administer panaceas that never quite deliver all that they promise is the desiccated academic approach to teacher improvement that is held together by such opaque language as to make it effectively useless to the busy teacher who just wants to know how to be better. How many of us have sat through a presentation from a university-based academic that was as far from real classroom life as Stockhausen is from Justin Bieber?[1] (Renowned physicist Richard Feynman tells the story of being fazed by a paper on sociology that contained such lines as, 'The individual member of the social community often receives his information via visual, symbolic channels' until he realised it meant, 'People read'. Interestingly there is research from Princeton University that shows that while undergraduates tend to write in a convoluted manner to appear more intelligent to the reader, this actually has the opposite effect. You can read all about this in a paper entitled, ironically, *Consequences of Erudite Vernacular Utilized Irrespective of Necessity*.)

Somewhere between these two positions you will also find the heated debate about the very nature of teaching itself and whether it is a) a trade; b) an art; c) a science; or d) all of the above. Any country facing a teacher shortage but not a children shortage will do its best to get adults in front of young people as quickly as possible, which paves the way for a more 'on the job' approach to teacher training. In other words, many teachers will be qualified just a couple of years after your child has left school[2].

Is teaching, then, a set of skills you learn, like being a plumber or a spot welder? Is it an art, something you are born to be, like becoming a dancer or a very good plumber? Or is it a science, akin to being a doctor, something for which you need

---

1   If you have to look up both of these musical greats then maybe you really are in the wrong job

2   One Tweet recently pointed out that training to teach in this way was like being in the 'Five items or fewer' queue at Tesco. You get there quicker but with less in your basket

years of training combining hands-on practice with sound academic theory and not killing anyone.

The answer, if we are honest, is all three. Which is why Zoë Elder's book has come along at just the right time in just the right way.

This is not a quick-fix book. At over 60,000 words it is very definitely not a handy pocket guide to improving your practice. There are enough of those out there as it is, getting 'the buggers' to read, write, think, behave or any number of active verbs we want children to do in class so we can teach them. Nor, though, is this book a heavy academic tome. Although it draws much of its wisdom from the research that is out there concerning the nature of high quality teaching and learning, it puts it across in a way that is clear, thorough and accessible (and, with Zoë's eye for design, beautifully presented).

What's more, it is a practical book full of ideas and tips drawn from Zoë's not inconsiderable time spent in the classroom as a teacher and advisor working with all sorts of children in all sorts of ways. 'Full on' is the best way we've found to describe the manner in which learning takes place in Zoë's lessons and, as books for teachers go, this a very full on book, as you would expect.

In a nutshell, what Zoë has done is to create a book that shows how teaching is a hands-on craft that can be enhanced through science and, when done well, is something of an art. What more can you want from a book that will help you become a seriously better teacher?

And how much more professionally gratifying than leaping on the next bandwagon that rolls up in your staffroom whilst the person in charge of CPD screams, 'All aboard!'

Ian Gilbert
Santiago
May 2012

TELL ME AND I'LL FORGET; SHOW ME AND I MAY REMEMBER;

INVOLVE ME AND I'LL UNDERSTAND.

Chinese proverb

CONTENTS

History unfolded differently on different continents because of differences among continental environments,

3   Diamond, J., *Guns, Germs and Steel: A Short History of Everybody for the Last 13,000 Years* (London: Vintage, 1998).

not because of biological differences among people.

Jared Diamond[3]

Before you build a boat you have to need a boat

Humans didn't have the idea of a boat until they came across a river that was too wide or a lake that was too vast to cross. They didn't *need* a boat until their environmental conditions determined that they required one. Once the circumstances changed, they applied ingenuity and practical reasoning to the problem. They got together, discussed and identified the key issues, tried stuff out, reflected upon it, made improvements and solved the problem. Then, and only then, did they build a boat.

Full On Learning is a way to tap into humanity's natural ability to build boats; to learn new things as a way of actively overcoming problems. It's something we've been doing for hundreds of thousands of years, something we are *well-practised at doing*. Full On Learning brings out that innate learning ability that *all* children have, regardless of their academic ability, and it does so in a way that is effective, motivating, enjoyable and intensely engaging.

The first stage in learning to build a boat is understanding the river. So, for learning to take place we first need a problem to solve or an issue to overcome. Fortunately, this is where the mess we are making of the planet comes in handy. Our world poses many challenges and undoubtedly there are many more just around the corner. What happens when coal runs out? Or oil? Or water? Or the sun? We may not know what the problems of the future will be, but we do know what skills and

3

dispositions we, or rather the children we are teaching, will need in order to undertake the vast array of problem-solving that the future will require.

This is what Full On Learning seeks to produce: capable and confident learners who are developing the skills, knowledge and dispositions to become capable and confident problem-solvers and leaders for a lifetime beyond school.

The Full On Learner:
a client brief

If we are to educate young people for the newly emerging global landscape there are only two things we can predict: the unpredictable and the unexpected. We could fill them with facts and test how well they have learned them, but in the meantime those self-same facts are becoming obsolete. Full On Learning isn't about children *not* acquiring knowledge; far from it. Knowledge is power and in order to build new things you need a foundation of old things, just as in Newton's famous quote about 'standing on the shoulders of giants'. But when it comes to the unpredictable and unexpected, the facts, if there are any, can be wrong. What young people really require is to be aware of how they need to *know and understand*, what they need to *be able to do* and how they need to *be*. This is my list which I think covers most bases:

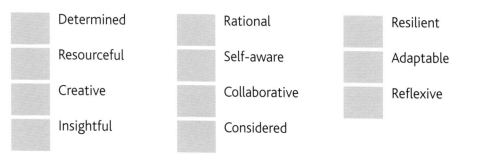

Determined	Rational	Resilient
Resourceful	Self-aware	Adaptable
Creative	Collaborative	Reflexive
Insightful	Considered	

If we send out into the world young people who have developed, practised and refined these characteristics as children then, although they may not be able to save the world, they will certainly be able to put up a pretty good fight.

Quality education needs to develop these characteristics in *every individual* learner, regardless of their academic ability. The only way to do this is to give them a rich diet of opportunities in which they get to deepen their levels of resilience, creativity, resourcefulness and so on. However, there is one further trait that all learners need to develop that does not appear on my list – the quality of discernment. This is the ability to make informed and appropriate decisions in a world that relentlessly presents choices and demands immediate responses. Just when we are starting to feel comfortable with the Information Age it is evolving into the Ideas Age. Information has been democratised. Anybody in the world with a computer and an internet connection has access to a wealth of knowledge – more than was imagined less than 50 years ago. They can download what is available and upload what they have, adding their own contribution to the global pool of information. They can do this wherever and whenever they want and as often as they like. It isn't knowledge that sets us apart these days; it's what we do with it. For today's young people, the world is their oyster – but only for those who position themselves ready to stand up, be counted and make a distinctive, discerning contribution.

Full On Learning provides a blueprint for teachers to methodically and artfully create opportunities for learners to flourish. In doing so, we, as educators, will develop a repertoire of techniques to support learner progress in all areas – explicitly to value, assess and celebrate newly acquired skills, dispositions and, yes, knowledge. And remember, in the same way as when early humans first stumbled across a new river and then discovered that trees float, there is space for surprises too. The joy of new challenges, of insightful observations, of unexpected outcomes and of that one student who rarely contributes in a discussion slowly lifting their hand for the first time.

> [A]ll behaviour is an interaction between nature and nurture, whose contributors are as inseparable as the length and width of a rectangle in determining its area.
>
> Steven Pinker[4]

I passionately believe that the ability to learn is not solely determined at birth (although the basic tools for learning do have a genetic element). Rather, it is the circumstances in which we find ourselves that have the greatest influence on the capacities we go on to develop and that enable us to reveal our talents.

What Full On Learning seeks to do is tap into all young people's innate ability to learn and give them a chance to show us (and themselves) what they can do with it.

Expert pedagogues

The roles and responsibilities of the 21st century teacher have attracted much discussion. In a world in which my 3-year-old goddaughter can confidently select and use applications on her dad's iPhone and, at the same time, perform confidently as party photographer with her mum's digital camera, the role of teacher as expert-imparter-of-knowledge is under pressure. But it is no less important; it's just that *what* teachers *do* must change and should continue to be able to change. It must.

Full On Learning asserts that the 'act' of teaching needs to be as expert an activity as it ever was. As teachers, just as with elite performers in sport, politics, science or the arts, we must unpick what it is that makes us 'expert' so that we can practise it carefully, mindfully and deliberately. After all, teaching is one of the most deliberately intrusive acts that we can carry out. When learners enter our classrooms or learning spaces, we are required to interrupt their conversations, thoughts and actions so that we can redirect their attention to what we need them to learn.

---

4   Pinker, S., *The Language Instinct: How the Mind Creates Meaning* (New York: Harper Perennial Modern Classics, 2000).

Every lesson is just such an intervention. It is a request for learners to plug in, switch on and actively respond to learning opportunities. Our teaching repertoire, therefore, needs to encompass a wealth of well-considered and thoughtful inter-ruptions. We must ensure that these intrusions really count – to be the Saatchi & Saatchi of learning in every conversation and activity we design. We need to perfect the channels through which great ideas emerge, spread and grow – from us to them and from them to us.

Learning is far too important to be left to chance

Looked at in this way, teaching can be viewed as a punctuation mark in the steady flow of semi-conscious and unconscious thoughts that run through a learner's mind. As such, we are in a fantastically powerful and influential position. And a very exciting one.

We need to be mindful about why, when and how we deliver our interruptions. Each and every one of them can make a 'learning difference' – learning that really sticks and has a life beyond the lesson. This is at the heart of Full On Learning: making sure that the actions we take, the lessons we plan, the activities we design and the language we use are *consciously* considered and deployed to the greatest effect. In this way we can pass on our own expert learning methodology to learners, so they can implement the same level of conscious thought in their own lives. As a result, they will have genuine control, real choice and purposeful direction when it comes to what they do, where they do it, who they do it with and, most importantly, the kind of people they become. They will be the discerning learners, leaders and citi-zens that the world needs.

The very best teaching practice always appears to be subtle, relaxed and inescap-ably 'natural'. As such, it would be easy to offer feedback about how marvellous the lesson was and how much progress the learners made, and then walk away, putting it all down to being in the presence of a gifted teacher. Full On Learning came about, however, from my conviction that teaching, like intelligence, is not fixed in a 'gifted' or 'not-so-gifted' system of talent-identification. It is not a question of random, unpredictable luck that contributes to making a great teacher. I believe that *all* teachers can sit proudly on the 'quality of outcome' line somewhere between 'good' and 'outstanding'. What's more, the position we find ourselves in on that line is not fixed. If we are honest we know that on some days we are great, on others, not so great. What is vital is that we continue to aspire to the levels of consistency displayed by the greatest performers – to become the McEnroe, Tendulkar or DuPre of teaching and learning. It is this consistency that sets the highest performers apart from the crowd.

To achieve this consistency of excellence, we have to unpick exactly what it is that characterises outstanding teaching; to spot it, analyse it and then replicate it. Just as I believe that all learners can develop, make progress and find new strengths and talents within themselves, we can do the same in our teaching practice and methodology. Time and time again, I have worked with teachers who, once given the opportunity to reflect on their own expertise and think of themselves as learners, immediately become far better placed to help others explore and develop the characteristics of excellent teaching for themselves.

Whenever I undertake an analysis of effective teaching practice, I am rewarded by the revelation of a highly complex and sophisticated web of deeply thoughtful, deliberate and mindfully designed interventions by the teacher. Full On Learning places that complex web under the microscope and analyses everything that underpins the most effective pedagogy. To examine each thread in turn is to enable all practitioners to sharpen, develop and reflect on their own practice. This makes the best learning accessible for everybody.

So, just take a look at any well-designed observation form to find the evidence of the direct, causal link between what the teacher does and says and how well learners learn. If learning is well designed, the observer will be able to make explicit links between everything the teacher does and how this directly impacts on the quality of learning. Everything a teacher does and says in the classroom counts. Full On Learning is about making sure it counts for the right reasons.

The three heart beats
of Full On Learning

 Every teacher action can have a direct causal effect on the quality of the learning experience. This brings with it a unique and exciting opportunity.

 As a result of the link between teacher action and learning outcomes, we know that *everything* we plan, do and say needs to be mindfully designed. Just as an architect considers the meticulous detail on a blueprint for a new building, so must we consider even the most subtle of our interventions. Every interruption we make has the power to change the course of our learners' personal learning journeys, for better or worse. It is probably this power of influence that keeps many of us in the profession.

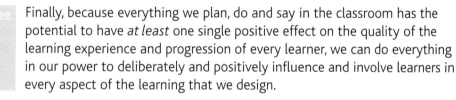 Finally, because everything we plan, do and say in the classroom has the potential to have *at least* one single positive effect on the quality of the learning experience and progression of every learner, we can do everything in our power to deliberately and positively influence and involve learners in every aspect of the learning that we design.

I'm not so naive as to believe everything will go according to plan. Once the lesson is designed and underway we also need to be able to adapt and respond to what is happening. If we can design learning so that it allows us to stand back and observe, we are very well placed to be able to act on the feedback we receive, address misconceptions and check out the knowledge and understanding presented by our learners.

Clearly, some things in a lesson will always remain beyond our control; there's no accounting for the windy Friday lunchtime that blows the students into your room in a perfect storm. All of which brings us back to the building of boats (sort of). It's worth remembering that the capacity for 'building boats' already exists within every learner before we even get started. The word 'educate' comes from the Latin *educere* meaning 'to draw out'. Full On Learning aims to do just that – to draw out the capacity for creativity, innovative thought, argument, discernment and curiosity that already exists by fostering an eagerness to learn and improve in our learners. This is what is meant by truly involving the learner in their learning.

The world into which we are sending our young people demands individuals who can collaborate and innovate, so we need to design explicit opportunities for students to practise team-working, rehearse idea-generation and test-out alternative approaches. To help them see the relevance of this, we must explain why we are doing so. We need to be clear about *why* we are asking them to construct their own problems to solve, and not simply answer a list of questions. If we want them to practise divergent thinking, we need to explain why reflecting and articulating their thinking to others is relevant. When we encounter the inevitable challenge, '... but what's this got to do with the exam?' we need to be ready with our rationale. Until, that is, this approach is so embedded in the learning culture that the students understand the relevance for themselves.

Digital learning capacities

The rapid integration of social networking and mobile technology provides a fantastic opportunity to both draw out and shape the innate capacities for learning in our learners. Digital technology presents infinite opportunities (of varying quality) to make sustainable learning connections and cross many boundaries. If we are really committed to nurturing discerning, enterprising, resilient and all-round savvy citizens, then there's a huge river of learning opportunities flooding into our schools. It is carried into our classrooms in the pockets of almost every student. Actively embracing the innovative use of technology to support learning is a brilliant way to involve, motivate and inspire our learners to engage with the world beyond their immediate horizons.

EFFECTIVE LEARNING SKILLS AND DISPOSITIONS	THE LEARNER …	THE TEACHER …
Collaborates	Analyses, critiques and questions their own and their peers' learning, always informed by their own expertise	Encourages learners to teach peers, older students and other groups and provides regular opportunities to work with a diverse group of learners and interested people beyond their peer group
	Grows their knowledge and understanding when they listen to different views and perspectives that challenge their thinking	Offers frequent opportunities for public presentations of understandings and peer review. Engagement in discussions, debate and with 'experts' in the field
Emotionally Intelligent	Feels safe to take learning 'risks'	Develops emotional learning abilities first, followed by intellectual and cognitive abilities by building learning communities
	Understands the need for learning in different ways, using various methods, groupings and resources and adapts well to these, even if they are unfamiliar to them	Communicates explicitly the 'why' of the learning to students, ahead of the 'how' and the 'what'. Feedback focuses on the 'struggle' in the learning, seeking to encourage strategies that overcome barriers to learning

EFFECTIVE LEARNING SKILLS AND DISPOSITIONS	THE LEARNER ...	THE TEACHER ...
Develops Expertise	Is self-aware, reflective and actively seeks to develop their skills and expertise Uses focused feedback from teachers and peers to develop their own expertise	Requires learning to be subjected to peer scrutiny so as to develop learners' intellectual resilience Encourages quality learning conversations, developing a reflection-centred classroom with an explicit focus on learning
Creative Thinker	Engages their imagination, creative thinking and capacity to question new and existing scenarios Creates new knowledge by making creative links between prior and present learning	Explicitly develops creative thinking through divergent thinking strategies, open-ended questions and challenges Draws on existing knowledge to apply to new situations and contexts through problem-solving tasks and makes new links
Involved	Knows exactly what their role as a learner entails Knows what they need to do to move from where they are to where they want to be	Regularly involves learners in the co-construction of the curriculum, learning intentions and success criteria Makes frequent and appropriate use of Assessment for Learning (AfL) curricular targets, Assessing Pupil's Progress (APP) and explicit Personal Learning and Thinking Skills (PLTS)/ learning dispositions so learners are clear about what they need to do to progress and can take responsibility for this

Digital	Articulates their thinking processes with their peers and with a global audience beyond the confines of their physical environment	Encourages frequent use of video-diaries, podcasting and learning journals that focus on the learning process rather than the learning product
	Is able to make informed decisions to select and analyse appropriate information and use tools that will enhance their learning	Provides opportunities for learners to scrutinise the use and application of digital technologies in learning
	Has the confidence to craft and safeguard a positive digital identity through considered contributions to the digital information space	Designs frequent learning opportunities that focus on developing quality contributions to the creation of new knowledge
	Is discerning in their assessment of and the comments that they make on the information presented in the digital world	Explicitly and regularly offers opportunities for reflection by learners on the quality of information presented in the digital world, and that which they contribute
Responsive to feedback	Deliberately practises their own expertise within and beyond school	Offers a varied diet that develops specific skills in different contexts, with different team members at different times
	Believes that they get better through hard work, not luck. Sets their own targets and believes they can always improve	Praises effort within a task rather than the individual attainment of the learner ('Clever is what clever does')
	Uses focused feedback from teachers, parents and peers to develop their own expertise	Actively promotes quality learning conversations, developing a reflective-centred classroom focused on learning

EFFECTIVE LEARNING SKILLS AND DISPOSITIONS	THE LEARNER …	THE TEACHER …
Powerful Learning Capacities	Ensures learning is personal to them. Is able to draw on experiences from the wider world beyond the classroom and the school to enhance their personal development	Makes it safe and appropriate for learners to refer to and share their own experiences, objects of importance and memories
	Is able to make informed choices about what, how, who with and when they are going to learn	Co-designs tasks, projects and activities with the learners. Holds the learners to account according to agreed success criteria
	Is confident in presenting ideas, thoughts and learning with peers and wider audiences. Responds actively and positively to feedback	Designs frequent and varied opportunities for learners to present their learning – both outcome and process. Classroom displays show the learning that is valued (e.g. drafts, amendments, changes, adaptations). Presentations of understanding are regular occurrences, with the whole school and wider community invited in to celebrate learning
Curious and questioning	Chooses to commit their time and effort to investigating aspects of their learning that they enjoy and find interesting and challenging, because they are driven by curiosity about the world in which they live	Designs learning challenges that are peppered with questions and provide ample opportunities for discussion, debate and investigation

	Learner	Teacher
	Thrives when faced with unfamiliar ideas, objects and challenges. Actively engages in discussion/debate through listening and contributing ideas, reflecting on own and other's contributions and summarising pertinent points	Establishes an environment of curiosity. Embraces new technologies, artefacts and objects as part of a culture of the 'learning exploratory'. Employs anticipation as an effective part of building and excitement in learning
	Asks quality questions that reflect higher order thinking (speculation, hypothesising and knowledge-creation) and structures enquiry routes	Designs thinking and enquiry frameworks to support learner enquiry and promote investigative thinking. Develops agreed success criteria with learners to assess the quality of questions posed
Motivated	Chooses to commit their time and effort to tasks they enjoy, find interesting and challenging because it matters to them	Designs learning challenges that are relevant to now and the future and have a clear purpose
	Grows their knowledge and understanding when they listen to different views and perspectives that challenge their own thinking	Offers frequent opportunities for public presentations of understandings and peer review. Engagement in discussions, debate and with 'experts' in the field
Learning Entrepreneurs	Enjoys finding unconventional methods and processes to gain new knowledge and skills	Integrates choice at a variety of levels into tasks. Learning processes are acknowledged alongside learning outcomes
	Manages risk well in challenging situations and tasks. Is prepared to 'go out on a limb' and responds positively to setbacks, eager to learn from these and plan and take the next steps	Encourages learners to take responsibility for learning opportunities at appropriate times

Never doubt that
a **small** group of
thoughtful, committed people
can **change** the world.
Indeed, it is the **only**
thing that ever has

Margaret Mead

LEARNERS WHO ...	TEACHING THAT ...
Analyse, critique and question their own and peers' learning, always informed by their own expertise	Encourages learners to teach peers, older students and other groups and provides regular opportunities to work with a diverse group of learners and interested people beyond their peer group

Focus: Collaboration |
| Grow their knowledge and understanding when they listen to different views and perspectives that challenge their own thinking | Offers frequent opportunities for public presentations of understandings and peer-review. Engagement in discussions, debate and with 'experts' in the field

Focus: Presentations of understanding |
| Are self-aware, reflective and actively seek to develop their skills and expertise | Requires learning to be subjected to peer scrutiny so as to develop intellectual resilience

Focus: Peer-assessment |

COLLABORATION

Why collaborative learning is important for us all

Humans are social beings and we like to interact – to share ideas and receive positive feedback and affirmation for our achievements. Many of us actively seek out such opportunities for interaction with others. The explosion of social networking is evidence enough for that.

But it is worth remembering that even the most confident individual can be eye-wateringly shy when it comes to unfamiliar social situations. Luckily, we learn how to behave in such situations and build up experiences that feed our confidence. We develop strategies, learning from the mistakes we have made, to understand what is expected of us in social settings. The point is that we learn the subtle rules of interaction over time.

It is easy to forget that, in comparison to adults, our learners have a very modest experience of social interactions. Yet they are required to interact in a plethora of unfamiliar and challenging contexts throughout the school day. From one lesson to the next, particularly in secondary schools, they are asked to get into groups of four or five, into pairs, or work with '... somebody they've never worked with before' or simply look around the class and find a partner for themselves. Even the most socially hardened adult would find this challenging. If you've ever had the chance to shadow a student, you'll know by about the second or third lesson just how exhausting this can be.

So this chapter is all about what great collaborative learning looks, sounds and feels like. It gives the key ingredients to build into learning design as well as some useful indicators to assess how well it's going. Most importantly, this will provide you with a way to highlight, for the learners and yourself, the *progress* every learner makes in any collaborative learning situation.

This chapter looks at how we can help our learners when they find themselves in group situations of our design and give them the language and the opportunity to reflect on how they need to *be* when they are learning collaboratively. It suggests ways in which we can *deliberately* provide learners with opportunities to think *explicitly* about how an effective group member actually behaves. We only have to think about the stresses that surround the organisation of any social gathering to know that collaboration and productive interaction don't happen by chance. Everybody involved has to work at it.

But the issue for us, as teachers, is where to begin.

Deliberately designing opportunities for learners to learn how to think and generate ideas *together* is particularly important in light of the way that technology is shaping our working lives. The information age has brought collaborative learning centre stage. We need to support young people in the development of interpersonal and intra-personal skills and dispositions. So we need to give learners regular opportunities to practise the skill of listening to – and being challenged by – others, of experiencing critical feedback and of accepting praise. The rapidly increasing connectivity that exists across the globe means that being able to communicate and work effectively with others will surely be a defining characteristic of the successful citizen of the 21st century and beyond. And with almost 7 billion people inhabiting the world, that's a lot of collaboration.

What is the focus for this lesson?

If we consider group work as a powerful tool for learning, then the natural question as we start our planning is, 'How will learning in groups ensure progression?' or, put simply, 'Why do it this way?' We often get challenged by this very question by the learners themselves when we organise them into their groups. It is worth rehearsing what our rationale is for setting up the learning in this way. The table below gives a quick checklist to help structure groups according to the purpose of learning.

When we trust people, conversation, discussion and the sharing of ideas flows – and flows quickly. Without trust, we can be distracted by preconceived ideas, unfounded low expectations and most likely fear. As a result, learning and development can be inhibited. If we build trust into the communities and groups in which we learn and work then the learning will be deeper and more sustained.

The characteristics of effective collaboration

One of the most beneficial aspects of collaborative learning is the space it provides for the explicit development of learning competencies and dispositions. Using the principle of the 'wisdom of crowds', the group can provide all the subject-specific clarification required to complete the challenge. What requires deeper reflection and skill is the *process* by which the group completes the challenge. This is where you, as the expert pedagogue, step in. From the moment that the challenge is designed to the moment at which learners get to evaluate the why, the how and the what[5] of their learning, your skill will allow the group to value the way in which

---

5   The 'Why' 'How' 'What' approach that I talk about is adapted from an engaging business leadership model presented by Simon Sinek in his TEDxPuget Sound Talk (17th September 2009). I first watched it here http://www.youtube.com/watch?v=u4ZoJKF_VuA&feature=relmfu. Simon Sinek also has a great website http://www.startwithwhy.com/and a book, *Start with Why?* http://www.amazon.co.uk/Start-Why-Leaders-Inspire-Every-one/dp/0241958229/ref=sr_1_1?ie=UTF8&qid=1317915333&sr=8-1. His book and website reinforce the model. Here, the concept he talks about is more fully explained: http://www.startwithwhy.com/Learn/Glossary1.aspx?letter=Golden%20Circle

From the website: 'Golden Circle - The model that codifies the three distinct and interdependent elements (Why, How, What) that makes any person or organization function at its highest ability. Based on the biology of human decision making, it demonstrates how the function of our limbic brain and the neocortex directly relate to the way in which people interact with each other and with organizations and brands in the formation of cultures and communities.' The concept is fully explained in Simon Sinek's book, *Start With Why*, published in 2009.

N.B. I've adapted this model in a lot more detail in Chapter Two: Emotionally Intelligent Learners.

they learned alongside what they learned. In doing so, you get to make these valuable learning skills and dispositions explicit.

If we design learning opportunities that deliberately and explicitly foster the character traits of an 'effective learner', then learners can mindfully practise them. For example, if we deliberately design opportunities for students to develop their ability to work in teams *and* share this intention with them *and* design ways in which we might specifically assess how well they progress against our stated intentions, then the chances are that our actions will have a direct and positive impact on how well they develop these collaborative skills.

Watch any episode of Big Brother, The Apprentice or Strictly Come Dancing and you will see that collaboration doesn't 'just happen' – far from it. So although I began this chapter with the statement 'Humans are social beings', it doesn't mean that we all get on when we are thrown into a group of strangers. We all need to practise our team-working skills and consider exactly what it is we need to do and be like in any group scenario before we get really good at team tasks. This is no different for the young people we teach. In fact, with all the growing up they are busy doing, they could be forgiven for being a little distracted when it comes to learning collaboratively with their peers.

Explicit opportunities to practise collaboration

The discrete opportunities we can give to learners will allow them to deliberately practise the characteristics of being an effective learner, such as creative thinking, evaluation, strategic planning and collaboration. It is this purposeful practice that is critical to developing expertise and echoes the work of Anders Ericsson who famously identified the 10,000 hours rule that can be applied to how we approach the development of Full On Learners in the 21st century.[6]

If the learners of today are the voters, decision-makers and leaders of tomorrow, they need to practise their ability to be discerning in the company of friends, colleagues and online communities. We all have varying levels of discomfort when we are asked to work in groups; just mention 'role play' and many of us will run a mile.

Perhaps the truth of the matter is that the adult who says, 'I don't like working in groups' is the child who never got the opportunity to practise and learn how to. Or maybe they were the adult for whom working in groups has *never* suited their preferred learning style. In both cases, that's okay; so long as we are aware of this and can honestly respond to the following question: How do you ensure that your own preferred learning style (of working independently) doesn't prevent you designing regular opportunities for all your students to practise working in groups?

In terms of thinking collaboratively or solving problems in groups, quite often the opportunities to practise what this entails can be few and far between. Effective Full On Learners happily embrace collaborative challenges.

---

6 Ericsson, K. A., Prietula, M. J. and Cokely, E. T., The Making of an Expert. *Harvard Business Review* 85 (7/8) (2007): 114–121. Available at http://www.coachingmanagement.nl/The%20Making%20of%20an%20Expert.pdf.

Sam's YouTube collaboration

Consider our *fictional* student, Sam, who is 8 years old. For as long as he can remember, he has danced to whatever music he has heard on the TV, radio or MP3 player. His parents have encouraged him to show off his talents at Christmas and birthday parties. Sam is very used to performing for others, and not just those within his immediate world. For the past year, he has used his mobile phone to film himself, upload this onto the family computer and onto his own YouTube channel. Not only that, but Sam has learned from other dancers of all ages and backgrounds by seeking out other people's dancing videos. Sam is now an active member of a global community of self-taught and self-improving dancers. It is this community that serves as the life-blood of Sam's emerging talent. And Sam, at age 8, is pretty good. And he knows it. He knows it because he can see it when he compares his abilities with others, and when he shows off his latest dance moves at school, he finds himself having to teach them how to do it. But most of all, he knows just how good he is because his YouTube dance community tell him so through the instantaneous feedback he receives from them every time he uploads a new video.[7]

---

7   This adapted fictional account is inspired by a short story re-told by Chris Anderson, founder of TED, in his 'How YouTube is driving Innovation' http://www.youtube.com/watch?v=LnQcCgS7aPQ&feature=iv&lr=1&user=TEDtalksDirector& src_vid=X6Zo53M0lcY&annotation_id=annotation_962757

Collaborative peer learning

For young people, YouTube presents an opportunity to amplify their interests and showcase their abilities to a global audience. In the early years of today's primary schools there are children who can be classed as Generation AYT (After YouTube) who were born in or after 2005 – the year that YouTube first went live. This means that for their entire lives the digital world has given them a public platform to showcase their talents, receive immediate global comment and the facility to respond to this feedback.

We know that powerful learning happens when we receive effective feedback – which tells us where we are, what we have done well and what we need to do next to build on our achievements. Collaborative learning provides the ideal forum for the feedback to flow backwards and forwards, from learner to learner, from learner to teacher, from teacher to learner. Sam's experience captures a rich online learning experience but, in truth, the qualities of his learning experience can be replicated in any collaborative learning opportunity that you design.

What can we learn about great collaboration from the YouTube experience?

From the example of Sam's YouTube experience, his community of YouTube dancers has become his principal 'teacher'. This illustrates the key components of some of the most powerful collaborative learning and how it can be designed to motivate and engage our learners:

1. **Safe learning.** As with all the best learning – and one of the central messages of Full On Learning – this doesn't 'just happen'. In the same way we would instruct Sam how to play safely with friends in the local park, he has to learn how to be safe online. He needs to be taught how to be discerning, to make informed decisions, to identify those things that are unfamiliar, to know what to do if he feels uncomfortable and to have access to e-safety tools. His parents/carers need to ensure that all of this is in place for his first supervised outings online. Collaborative learning behaviours, whether in the classroom, on a field trip or online, need to be learnt, practised and

developed. Only then will Sam be able to get the most out of the learning opportunities that the class of YouTube now offer him.

2 **Belonging**. His classroom is his online community. He has a strong sense of belonging to this community of dancers. This is one of the central pillars of his motivation and ability to learn.

3 **Efficacy**. Sam can exercise complete control over who can comment on his performance, what he wishes to respond to and what he wants to watch and learn from.

4 **Choice**. Sam can make selections about what he chooses to watch (with parental controls in place) and what he chooses to share. If anybody posts an inappropriate comment, his e-safety awareness will allow him to take appropriate steps to tell an adult and calmly block them if necessary. He can (through agreement with his parents) select when, where and how he practises/learns and for how long. He is, in truth, designing his own curriculum, according to his own needs and learning goals.

5 **Informed feedback**. Sam's online collaboration provides him with expertise, critical appreciation and encouragement. By presenting what he can do publicly, he receives instantaneous feedback.

6 **Mindful modelling**. Through observing others, Sam refines, adapts and improves his technique. There is not one single imparter of great knowledge for the young dancer but, instead, a collaborative pool of expertise from which he is able to watch, learn, adapt and select. The teaching behaviour of the online community is all about mutual appreciation.

7 **Expert input**. Through this community, Sam can see some of the most innovative techniques currently being performed. These may be skills that he would not be able to access from his immediate physical environment. Added to this is the fact that he can also watch traditional dancers and styles from different cultures and the 'greats' from archive collections and learn from them.

8   **Gallery of learning.** Every time Sam uploads a new video, he gets to experience a sense of achievement through sharing his development and progress with his community. He shows others what he is able to do. He celebrates his progress in its own right and the community encourages him to continue to do this.

Although this scenario is fictitious, it is a fiction based on the culture of learning that is happening every day for many, although by no means all, of our learners. For some of them, it is an incredibly familiar component of their lives beyond the formal curriculum and the normal school day. Full On Learning seeks to tap into *all* the things that make learners tick to make learning relevant and powerful, not simply in terms of content, but in the ways in which they see and experience the world. How much more powerful and sustainable would Sam's progress be if all of the above is replicated when Sam comes into your lesson tomorrow? What if you design learning around these collaborative principles to allow Sam to get to grips with his latest science project? How might you design learning in Sam's next lesson so that he and his peers can thrive in a physical collaborative environment that shares all the characteristics of powerful learning with which he is familiar?

In this way, even the *style* and *design* of the collaborative learning opportunities we offer can be truly relevant to learners and help us blur the boundaries for them between the formal and informal curriculum – making learning truly Full On.

Collaborative learning pedagogy

If you need further evidence that the school community *really* matters to learners like Sam, check out the story of the YouTube 'vodcasting' phenomenon Nicholi White.[8] The lip-syncing videos created by this 13-year-old boy in his local Apple store went viral within a few months, resulting in parallel online and 'real' notoriety. When interviewed about his sudden fame, his response reflects all you need to

---

8   See http://www.youtube.com/user/nicholifavs.

know about the influence and importance of teachers, 'I'm going back to school on September 9th and I can't wait. I'm going to show my teachers.'

Nicholi's collaborative online community provide him with overwhelming validation of his talent, but the recognition that he truly seeks is that of his immediate and local community of peers and teachers. Such is the power of community in all that we do. Being able to share our successes and have our gifts and talents publicly affirmed by the people with whom we have personal relationships and interact with on a daily basis is critical to our self-confidence and aspirations. But none of this is exclusive to the online world. The skills required to collaborate are generic, so if we give learners the opportunities to develop them in our lessons, they are going to have a good chance to interact and collaborate in the blurred world of the 21st century online/offline environment.

Building secure and supportive communities is fundamental to Full On Learning. We can only learn when we feel safe to do so. The best kind of learning has an 'emotional tag' and we want that tag to be as positive as possible to make sure the learning sticks. As teachers, we need to invest time, energy and expertise in the creation of classroom collaboration, where learners can rehearse in a safe, low-risk environment the skills required to be effective team-workers.

Collaborations provide learners with a gallery for their rich diversity of gifts, talents and abilities. The learning communities we design should give their passions a space to be expressed and a voice to be heard. Sam finds his audience on YouTube and thereby a space for his voice online. Nicholi White did the same. In lessons, we need to establish a culture where there are many spaces for learners to share their progress and their products of learning. Because what really matters to any learner is the reception they get from those closest to them in a *real* and human space.

The design and delivery of collaborative learning

When it comes to collaborative learning opportunities in our lessons, there are a number of components that we can be very deliberate about. Learners need to practise learning together, developing their skills and the learning dispositions of empathy, sensitivity, determination and resilience. We can make the development of these skills explicit through our learning objectives and success criteria by exploring the specific question of, 'What makes a good or effective group member?' alongside curriculum-specific objectives.

1 **Build communities**. In deference to our emotional needs, we must deliberately design community-building activities that foster a sense of safety and belonging ahead of any activity. Often, through nobody's fault, the timetable presents us with an obstacle to spending time on building communities and to do so might feel like an indulgence. Consistently, however, I have experienced that the time and effort I invest in building a learning community is paid back in full and with interest. Once established, nurtured and sustained, learning happens at a far deeper level and often with an accelerated rate of progression for all learners. Be aware that you may worry you are spending too much time 'just talking' and not enough time 'doing' or covering enough 'stuff' but over a period of just a few sessions, you will become part of a dynamic, highly sophisticated group of reflective practitioners and learners. The establishment of a safe learning community enables everybody to make huge gains in their thinking and, as a result, their progress.

2 **Be a coach**. Every time we address a group as a whole, we become, momentarily, a member of that group. There's no such thing as an outsider when we're developing a collaborative learning culture. As such, every time we intervene, we alter the group dynamic. One way of preventing this is to stand back and observe. We can then provide feedback from a distance and in a focused and specific way.

3   Explain the 'how'. When we set up the groups we need to make sure we get them to consider *how* they are going to work together in addition to *what* they need to do. This will avoid them listening to the task, seeing what they have to do, setting off followed by a rash of hands flying up to ask how to do it.

4   Deliberately plan interventions to ensure they count. The power of effective feedback can never be underestimated. The key is to ensure that the feedback channel is pointed in the right direction – from learner to teacher. For learners to progress in every lesson, we need to check understanding and address misconceptions and inaccuracies. The quickest way to do this is by listening and observing learning as it takes place. In this way, we can adapt our teaching style immediately and provide learners with an alternative way of doing things. If we choose to intervene and disrupt the learning flow, we need to make sure it really counts.

5   Exploit the power of the sticky note. Use sticky notes (or other 'feedback wall' strategies) wherever possible. This allows the learning to continue without interruption, so it is only at those times chosen by the learners that our feedback is included in their thinking.

> These notes can be placed on the desk of the learner or on an 'observation wall' and can be used as the script for progress checks and plenaries during the lesson. If the teacher makes sure that they make a specific comment on the learning of every learner in the room over one or a series of lessons, by naming each note/comment then it's another way to build a sense of community with the group.

> If learners are working in groups, a role for one group member could be 'Feedback monitor'. They have to collect feedback from the wall/teacher during the session and make sure it gets back to their group members.

> Give the sticky notes to the learners. They can then pose their own questions during collaborative learning activities and the teacher

can have a 'conversation' with them via the sticky note, without interrupting the thinking of everybody else.

In addition, the notes can be compiled into an FAQ board of some sort and learners can be tasked with providing the answers for each other – another way of keeping the energy for learning in the hands of the learners.

6 **Ask, don't tell.** When we do speak to the students, rather than telling them what they need to do next, we can shape our language to be questioning and coaching, so we prompt them to think more deeply, reconsider or try an alternative.

7 **Plan groupings according to learning purpose.** Learners are often asked to work in groups that are not concerned with the purpose or intended learning outcome. Effective group work is underpinned by deliberate planning of group formation. It is hard to design tasks that are genuinely 'group tasks', where all learners get to contribute according to their learning needs and abilities. A general rule of thumb when it comes to who goes where is that diverse groups tend to accommodate open-ended tasks, where enquiry skills are required. In this way, learners can pursue their own interests in their preferred learning style and bring what they have discovered back to the whole group. Diverse groupings also support problem-solving activities, where the 'two/three/four/five heads are better than one' really does prove to be true. In a problem-solving task, the best approaches are often produced as a result of the collation of a range of perspectives and interpretations.

When launching divergent thinking activities to generate a wealth of ideas – where quantity is sought over quality – groupings of different types of thinkers will work well. This is also true of learning tasks where a new concept is being introduced. At this introductory stage in the learning process, there is safety in knowing that although the concept is new to you, everybody in the group is in the same boat. On the other hand, when a specific skill is being developed, it is helpful to create similar ability groupings to maintain the sense of mutual support and positive peer influence. Where a common interest is being explored, you can promote deeper thinking

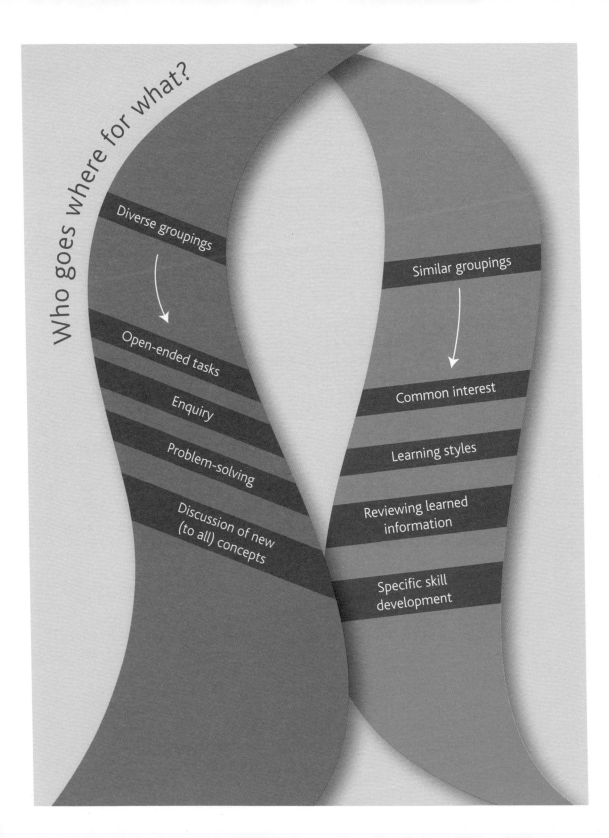

within a group who are at a similar stage in their understanding and skill development. This is also true of revision and consolidation activities. This also reduces the level of emotional and intellectual risk within the group, promoting positive attitudes to learning.

8 **Assign roles.** Ensuring that every member of the group has a specific job provides all learners with a reason to engage and contribute. Assigning roles prevents students hiding, coasting or being dumped with everything to do. Furthermore, if we have to ask learners to assign roles, we also have to plan authentic group tasks in the first place. In other words, we can use role assignment to quality assure the richness of the task. It also helps with the design of challenging learning opportunities and the clarification of success criteria.

9 **Be the observer.** Another benefit is the fact that once the groups have their roles, your role will revert back to coach and observer of learning. As such, you will be able to make notes, provide non-intrusive feedback and develop quality learning conversations with students.

10 **Lead reflection.** A striking aspect of great collaborative learning involves skilful leadership of reflective thinking. It would be fair to say that reflexive thinking (thinking ahead, through and back) pervades the learning environment. Written observations during the group work phase are integral to facilitating this process – modelling it for the learners and communicating this as an expectation of how learning should happen. Managing collaborative learning can be a challenge on a number of levels. Good task design is clearly crucial to the progress learners make during the lesson and is also central to the role that we adopt. A well-constructed collaborative task will clarify the what, the why and the how of learning. This will be coupled with an appropriate level of intellectual challenge and emotional safety in the configuration of the groups. With these key elements in place, we can take the lead in modelling reflective thinking.

 Identify quality. One of the main benefits of collaborative learning is the quality of the learning conversations that take place. We need to ensure we emphasise and clarify *what* the groups are being asked to do, *how*

they will do it and what *success* will look like. It is this final question that enables everybody involved to recognise and deepen their understanding of the learning outcomes. Lead this discussion ahead of any practical activity and, in doing so, you'll be able to ensure that all learners have a clear understanding of the learning to come. You can then employ your relentless questioning strategies to ensure that the pre-agreed success criteria are foremost in their thinking.

12 **Make progress visible.** Throughout collaborative learning sessions, build in structured opportunities for the groups to publicly show their learning to their peers, whatever stage they are at. The messier their thinking the better, as this is a great way to alert them to recognising the progress they are making and encourage them to take the lead in what happens next. Insisting that the groups show and explain their learning during the lesson reinforces the importance of the *process* of learning as well as the *product*. I have heard this referred to as the 'POP' of learning ('Process Over Product'). It also takes the pressure off the 'big reveal' moment at the end of the lesson, leaving space for mistakes to be celebrated as learning milestones in

what does a quality group member sound like?

what does a quali

what d

what difficulties might we face and what do we need to do when this happens?

what do we already kno

what will a quality 'product' look like?

their own right. Your expert skill will come to the fore when you draw out from these moments the integral components of the learning process and reflect them back to the learners as a whole group. They can then use each other's experiences to clarify their own understanding, address any inaccuracies or misconceptions and move their thinking forward.

13 **Keep quality at the heart of the learning.** Display the quality criteria of the group challenge in as many ways as possible and so it can be seen from all angles around the room. Encourage learners to refer to these at regular intervals (using sticky notes or a feedback wall) to ensure they are all on track (it can be one of the roles in the group to do just this).

One way of checking out the quality of collaborative learning in lessons is to try some of the practical strategies in the table on pages 36-37. Designing learning with these enquiry questions can form the basis of some great conversations about 'group work' as part of professional reflection and development.

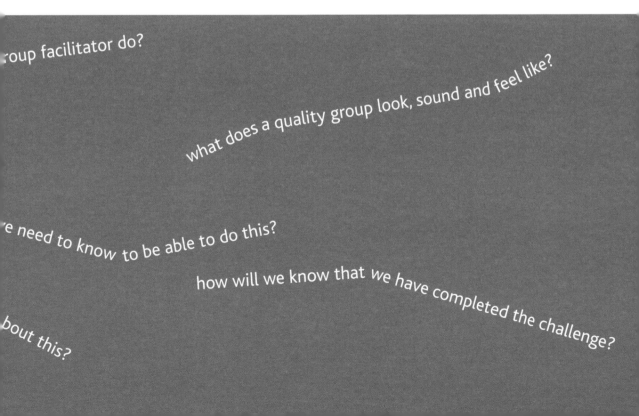

roup facilitator do?

what does a quality group look, sound and feel like?

e need to know to be able to do this?

how will we know that we have completed the challenge?

bout this?

Action Research

ENQUIRY QUESTIONS	FOCUS ON	PRACTICAL STRATEGIES
How can I create a sense of community in large groups of learners?	Regular check-ins with the group. Ensure learning talk characterises learning (regular opportunities to discuss, problem-solve and share ideas)	Creative starters requiring pairs into small groups then whole group thinking. Explicit discussion about 'What/who makes an effective group?' Design deliberate opportunities for a blend of divergent and convergent thinking activities. Invite the group to redesign the physical learning space to enhance effective discussion and sharing of ideas
How can I construct quality collaborative learning opportunities?	Project design with explicit roles assigned to learners to work on over longer periods of time with frequent opportunities for public sharing of progress	Design of longer-term projects and rich challenges using compelling questions and problems worth solving. Ask learners to construct the detail of the problems to be solved and then act accordingly. Discussion of success criteria for group work. What does each role have to do well? What will success in this challenge look, sound and feel like? Process check-ins where learners reflect on how they are doing against the success criteria and are able to seek advice from others on what they need to do next

ENQUIRY QUESTIONS	FOCUS ON	PRACTICAL STRATEGIES
What does a really good quality collaborative learning opportunity look, sound and feel like?	Observe learners, focusing on learning behaviours, quality of discussion and frequency of questions	Teacher as observer: 1 Use sticky notes to record memorable conversations, moments and actions that progressed each group's learning journey 2 Tally chart of questions asked by members in the group – reflection focused on 'What makes a quality question?' 3 Equal assessment value placed on skills, knowledge acquisition and disposition development

... don't assume

Sgt Miles Elder

Feel safe to take learning 'risks'. They ask questions, make suggestions, consider alternatives and actively seek opportunities to test and challenge themselves

Develops emotional learning abilities first; this is then followed by intellectual and cognitive abilities

**Focus: Building a learning community
Readiness to learn (and make mistakes)**

– – –→ EMOTIONALLY INTELLIGENT LEARNERS

Are you happy to jump in?

Taking a Full On approach to lesson design results in the integration of positive emotional tags for the learner. Intellectual risk-taking only happens if we feel emotionally secure to take a chance on getting something wrong. Encouraging intellectual risk-taking requires that all learners (and their teachers!) are feeling emotionally secure enough to put their hand up, make a suggestion or offer their precious idea in front of everybody else. This requires us to design learning that accommodates the emotional learning needs of everybody in the group. No small challenge, admittedly. If we get it right, however, positive participation will feel really good and this will ensure that learning has a genuine chance to *stick*. This chapter provides ways in which we can design learning so that it offers truly compelling and safe learning opportunities that are characterised by learners' readiness to roll their intellectual sleeves up, take a risk and jump in.

According to neuroscience[9], when we encounter new surroundings, respond to others or tackle new experiences, one of the first parts of our brain to engage is the amygdala, buried deep inside the brain. It is linked to our emotional centre and has no capacity for language or ability to reason. It simply responds to its environment in a primitive and non-verbal way, ready to activate our fight or flight response. It is however, central to determining how we feel, respond and react. Long-term memory and emotion are inextricably linked, so our emotional reaction to a stimulus has the potential to last for a very long time. Our initial emotional responses become part of our most enduring memories. If a new experience makes us feel excited, positive and happy, then that connection or 'tag' is logged and preserved. Similarly, if an experience makes us feel scared, uncomfortable and unhappy, then that's how that particular memory will be 'tagged'. The power of all these emotional tags is that they have the ability to instantaneously transport us to another time, place or situation in the blink of an eye. Or the sniff of a room. The smell of floor polish always takes me back to my old school hall. I can hear the whirr of the floor polisher and see the parquet tiles laid out in perfect herringbone patterns. Most importantly, I feel what I felt then. All of this in one whiff of polish. Powerful stuff. It would follow, then, that if we deliberately design learning to trigger powerful and *positive* emotional connections for every learner, well, that's going to lead to some awesome learning.

Provide the 'why' of learning ahead of the 'how' and the 'what'

Emotional-learning isn't just about grabbing and holding learners' attentions in a positive way. It's also about being aware of the power of the emotional brain to shape or 'tag' our learning experiences. The emotional tag is something that we can incorporate into the design of lessons. We have to be aware of how we can deliberately prompt positive responses and, at the same time, deliberately avoid

---

9   Curran, A., *The Little Book of Big Stuff About the Brain* (Carmarthen: Crown House Publishing, 2008).

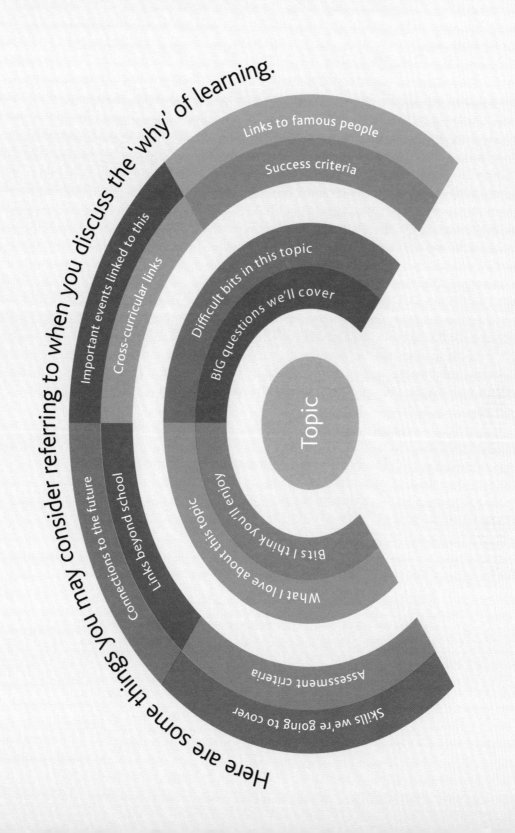

negative emotional tags. In his book, *Start with Why?*, Simon Sinek[10] talks about the need for businesses, brands and organisations to engage with our emotional self in the 'Golden Circle'. This is all about communicating the 'Why?' ahead of the 'How?' and the 'What?'. His contention is that many businesses have often only focused on the 'What?' in trying to engage with their clients. Only afterwards, have they talked about the 'How?' and then, in many cases, expected clients to work out the 'Why?' for themselves. He uses what we know about the brain, as previously described, to show why this approach often fails and he uses the example of Apple Computers and their incredible ability to nurture a loyal client base to explain what happens when it works. So what if we could use an adapted model to nurture our very own loyal and engaged groups of learners?

The first step to designing emotionally aware learning opportunities is to be explicit about *why*, *how* and *what* learners will be doing during your lessons. At a simple level, these three questions relate to the triune brain, where the why serves to address the survival needs of our reptilian brain, an engaging how keeps the emotional brain happy and the what can be addressed by our higher order thinking neo-cortex.

---

10 The 'Why' 'How' 'What' approach that I talk about is adapted from an engaging business leadership model presented by Simon Sinek in his TEDxPuget Sound Talk (17th September 2009).

I first watched it here http://www.youtube.com/watch?v=u4ZoJKF_VuA&feature=relmfu <http://www.youtube.com/watch?v=u4ZoJKF_VuA&feature=relmfu>

Simon Sinek also has a great website http://www.startwithwhy.com <http://www.startwithwhy.com/> /and a book, *Start with Why?* http://www.amazon.co.uk/Start-Why-Leaders-Inspire-Every-one/dp/0241958229/ref =sr_1_1?ie=UTF8&qid=1317915333&sr=8-1 <http://www.amazon.co.uk/Start-Why-Leaders-Inspire-Every-one/dp/0241958229/ref=sr_1_1?ie=UTF8&qid=1317915333&sr=8-1>. His book and website reinforce the model. Here, the concept he talks about is more fully explained: http://www.startwithwhy.com/Learn/Glossary1.aspx?letter=Golden%20Circle <http://www.startwithwhy.com/Learn/Glossary1.aspx?letter=Golden%20Circle>

From the Website: 'Golden Circle - The model that codifies the three distinct and interdependent elements (Why, How, What) that makes any person or organization function at its highest ability. Based on the biology of human decision making, it demonstrates how the function of our limbic brain and the neocortex directly relate to the way in which people interact with each other and with organizations and brands in the formation of cultures and communities.' The concept is fully explained in Simon Sinek's book, *Start With Why*, published in 2009.' Also included in previous footnote about Simon Sinek's work in the chapter on Full On Collaboration.

Why?

You'll know from your own experience that there's nothing worse than being asked to tackle a really difficult problem or complete an uncomfortable activity if we don't see the point of doing so. Research shows that intrinsic motivation is key to successful learning and, as such, we need to do everything possible to tap into it when we design learning opportunities.[11] One way to do this involves making the purpose and relevance of learning clear at the outset. Sharing the why is about the *really* big picture. It is where you get to communicate your passion about your subject, to make connections to prior learning and explore how this learning extends - and is relevant - beyond the school walls. The why of learning is connected to the success criteria of the learning tasks and the assessment objectives of the unit as a whole. In this way, you can build immediate and explicit milestones as progress measures for all learners in your lesson. One way to communicate the why of learning is to generate a mind-map of the topic you're teaching which makes the wider connections really explicit.

How?

This is where you get to share the way in which learning will happen. It is important that you design lessons that stimulate a range of positive emotions. Maybe you're asking students to work in groups or on their own. You might have a visitor coming in or perhaps you're asking them to present their ideas to each other. The 'how' is directly connected to the 'why' of learning.

What?

This is the content part – the topic, key questions, curriculum focus, new knowledge, skills and context. It is the part of the lesson that we're all really good at communicating and, interestingly, is the part we usually cover first.

With this approach, the 'what' deliberately gets shelved until last. Not only does this enable us to communicate the why first, but it also helps to trigger some important

11 Dweck, C. S. *Mindset, The New Psychology of Success* (New York: Random House, 2006).

emotional learning tags such as anticipation, eagerness and curiosity[12]. If we leave the 'what' until last, we are able to build anticipation of what we'll be doing *and* encourage learners to defer judgement at the same time. So you get multiple gains and benefits by planning in this emotionally aware way.

Enquiry-based learning

If we design our lessons by starting with the 'why', we can involve learners in constructing elements of the 'how' and the 'what' for themselves. One of the huge benefits of adopting an enquiry-based approach is precisely that it is a safe way to hand the learning over to the learners.

Here's an example – a little stylised maybe but you'll get the idea.

First, learners are presented with the 'why' and asked to respond directly to it:

'We believe that for you to be fully equipped for a world that has yet to be invented (by you) you need to be creative, work as part of a team, be articulate and confident. Most of all, we want you to develop a passion for learning and here's an opportunity to do just that.'

Next the 'how', which is the basic project structure (in this case, an enquiry-based team project with a timeline):

'So for the next few sessions, you'll be working with people you've never worked with before to help you develop your social learning skills and learn how to work as part of a team. You'll also be working in an entirely different setting with resources and tools that you may never have come across before. This will help you learn how to learn in new ways, in an unfamiliar setting and using different tools.

'You'll be deciding when to complete important parts of the task and who should be taking the lead for these (it's unlikely that this project can be

---

12 Curran, 2008, p81.

completed by one person alone – that's why you're in a team!). You're going to learn how to make decisions and you'll probably have some surprises along the way. This will enable you to experience and develop flexibility, creative thinking, working under pressure and the value of really great team-work.'

The 'what' can then be left to the learners themselves to decide, informed by assessment objectives and success criteria. We can provide supporting resources, plan a research visit, provide mentors or line up access to experts. They can construct their projects according to their interests and passions. The most important aspect of this style of learning design is that it is a fully emotional intelligent approach – each component designed to foster a sense of self-direction and self-efficacy - and, as such, provides the ideal space for intellectual risk-taking to be cultivated.

Habitat for ideas

There are many approaches and discrete whole-school programmes that aim to ensure a safe learning environment. At the heart of each is a recognition that we learn best when we feel safe to hypothesise, test out, explore and refute ideas in an effort to solve a problem. So that learning starts to look a bit like this:[13]

Real (problem-based) learning

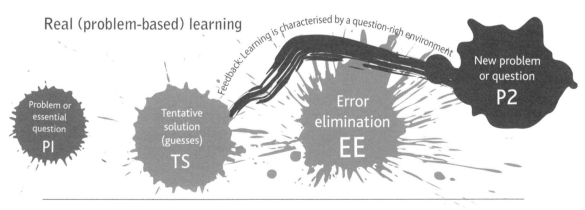

Feedback: Learning is characterised by a question-rich environment

Problem or essential question
PI

Tentative solution (guesses)
TS

Error elimination
EE

New problem or question
P2

13 Inspired by a keynote presentation by Professor Richard Bailey at National Association for Able Children in Education 11th Annual Conference for Local Authorities and Headteachers: 'Gifted and Talented: from Programme to Progress' November 29th 2010. http://www.richardbailey.net

Our skill as teachers enables us to set the tone and atmosphere of the lesson to allow this to happen. When teachers simply lead from the front, learners don't get to interact and will feel like they have no role other than as consumers of knowledge. Far more importantly, however, they don't get to try out ideas together as part of an exploratory learning community.

Ideas need to be tested and allowed to fail. They also need to be challenged and critiqued. Working within a safe community enables all learners to practise this process. Designing learning experiences around this results in a growth in intellectual capacity; the direct consequence of this is a learning community which is able and eager to learn in new contexts and with new people.

How old are you?

The easiest way to think about emotional security in learning is to reflect on the levels of maturity and thinking displayed by our learners. However, the way we tend to organise learning doesn't encourage us to do this: classes are grouped according to chronological age and, at times, may be subdivided into intellectual age (current or estimated levels of attainment). But what about our emotional age – how we feel when we are put in an unfamiliar situation? The high achieving student, whose credibility and identity is built on being successful at school, may struggle emotionally when faced with an activity for which he or she cannot guarantee a brilliant outcome. This may result in a half-hearted attempt at best and outright sabotage of the entire activity at worst. All because they don't feel safe enough to take an intellectual risk and give a different kind of learning a go.

IRT = EA (CA + IA)

Effective learners need a secure environment that will encourage them to go one (or more) step beyond what they usually expect or ask of themselves and each other. When we are engaging learners at any phase of education, learning that involves intellectual risk-taking (IRT) needs to connect with the emotional age (EA) of the learner first, rather than the chronological age (CA) or intellectual age (IA). This is not always easy, considering that the main thing we know about our learners is their year group. What we really need to know is:

- how well they cope with change

- how good they are at making and sustaining positive relationships with their peers

- how positive they feel about themselves and their levels of confidence, resilience and openness to new challenges, concepts and ideas

How well we are likely to learn is far better predicted by how we *feel* about our learning as opposed to how old we are and how well we have attained against others of a similar age. After all, how we feel will always come ahead of how we think, process and respond, so perhaps we can steal a competitive edge on behalf of our learners if we deal with what comes through the door first.

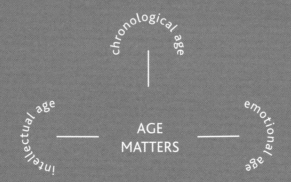

chronological age

intellectual age

AGE MATTERS

emotional age

We can find out about the emotional readiness of our learners by using an activity like the 'Are you ready to learn?' one below. I adapted this from two Independent Thinking colleagues who used a similar quick-fire questionnaire at a student conference to great effect (thank you, Roy Leighton and Dave Keeling). I usually use this to start a conversation about taking responsibility for learning under the heading of 'Whose learning is it anyway?' but it works in this context because it alerts the learner as to whether they are ready to learn or not. You can also use this in staff training, as it works really well for any reluctant learners you may have in your audience. Suffice to say, focusing on how learners are *feeling* about their learning at the beginning of a new topic or midway through is an incredibly powerful way to explicitly value their emotional state. At the same time, we accept that their emotional state is contextual and affected by moments in time (i.e. whatever they have just experienced) as well as how they feel about the new subject they are about to encounter.

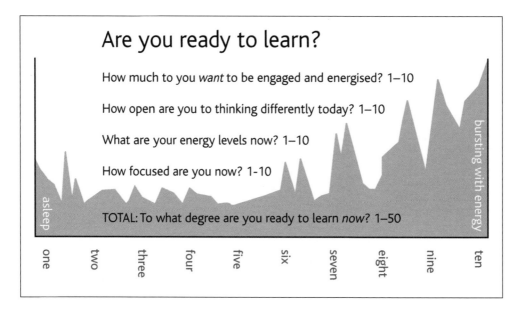

Are you ready to learn?

How much to you *want* to be engaged and energised? 1–10

How open are you to thinking differently today? 1–10

What are your energy levels now? 1–10

How focused are you now? 1-10

TOTAL: To what degree are you ready to learn *now*? 1–50

asleep

bursting with energy

one two three four five six seven eight nine ten

Once they have completed the self-assessment, ask them to add up their scores so they can rate themselves. Remember, this is a mere *snapshot* of how they are feeling about their learning at *this* moment and is not an indelible label (if you do this regularly they will get the point). The main thing to emphasise is that it is up to them to make the most out of their learning opportunities. Knowing ourselves is a powerful tool in our learning armoury . Being aware of how we are feeling is the first step to recognising how challenging (emotionally and intellectually) the learning is likely to be. Acting on it is the next step.

What does intellectual risk-taking look, sound and feel like?

We often hear about the need for educators to promote risk-taking in their lessons. If we are going to do this, we need confidence and courage to take risks in our lesson design. It's worth asking what 'risk-taking' might look, sound and feel like for our learners so we can spot it when it happens. After all, singing a song in public feels like a *huge* risk for one person while for another it is as easy as a stroll in the park.

There are three invaluable questions you can use to check if you had covered all emotional bases during your 'high-risk' lesson:

What did this look like?

Learners' body language was open

They used encouraging hand gestures towards each other when they were clarifying ideas

They made good eye contact with each other

They smiled

They were animated

What did this sound like?

There was a 'buzz'

All conversation within the groups was focused on the task at hand

They asked questions of each other and of the task

Their discussions used 'piggy-backing' to build a consensus

'Yes ... and ...' were used (rather than 'No ... but ...')

It was noisy (not rowdy)

3 **What did this feel like?**

For the teacher:

Freed up to observe, question and coach

Calm and secure

That they were in control of the direction of the task

For the learners:

They felt 'lost in discussion' and lost track of time

The lesson went quickly and they wanted to stay until they were finished

The bell annoyed learners because it stopped their thinking

Risk-taking goes both ways

The type of intellectual risk-taking behaviour that we can model and promote includes the following:

Stand back. For many of us, being quiet, stepping away from the reins and letting learners make their own discoveries (and 'mistakes'), will be the riskiest thing to do, particularly if there's somebody grading the progress of your learners. It's important to achieve a balance between 'developmental' observation and 'judgemental' observation. I heard one head teacher say recently that the more judgemental observations a teacher experiences, the 'worse' (more inhibited and controlling) they are likely to get. This is because we tend to revert to our 'safe defaults' when we feel that it's far too risky to innovate, let go and see what happens. If, on the other hand, we observe to develop practice and test out new ideas, then we can be encouraged to be enterprising and creative in our teaching and learners in their learning.

Demand *good* thinking. If learners are to make progress, they have to experience a change in their thinking. From the moment they enter the lesson, they need to think, consider, explore, puzzle and probe to make discoveries that will lead them to take something new (knowledge, understanding, insight, skills, abilities, capacities, etc.) away from your lesson. Ensuring that this progress is significant and meaningful requires us to pose questions and tasks that are authentically challenging. To do this, we need to think about what learners will find difficult and start from there as the entry point to the curriculum.

Ask, don't tell. When the moment of struggle surrounds our learners, we have a critical decision to make: provide or hold back. It may feel dangerous not to give a solution to a learner when they are clearly struggling, or to respond to a solution-seeking question by asking another question, but, by holding back, we leave the job of learning in the hands of the learner. The 'riskiest' questions from us might start to sound a lot like coaching questions:

'How might you find that out?'

'What will it look like when you've completed it?'

'Who else in the class might be able to help you with this (other than me)?'

'What else could you try to be able to solve this one?'

'What did you do last time you got stuck?'

'What alternative ideas could you come up with?'

In the world as uncertain as it is and as uncertain as it is likely to be ...

... continuing to do the same things in the same way ...

... could turn out to be the riskiest thing we do.

The safe learning lab

Once our emotional memory tags are imprinted in our brains they are incredibly hard to shift, particularly if those tags are negative. Effective learners have a wealth of positive emotional tags attached to their learning. When faced with a new challenge, their response is to feel excited because their prior experience of learning novel things has told them that this will be stimulating, enjoyable and rewarding. If learners feel sufficiently emotionally safe they will make suggestions, try out new ideas and inevitably make mistakes. It is only through the elimination of misconceptions, errors and inaccuracies that we learn anything – but this is often the toughest bit.

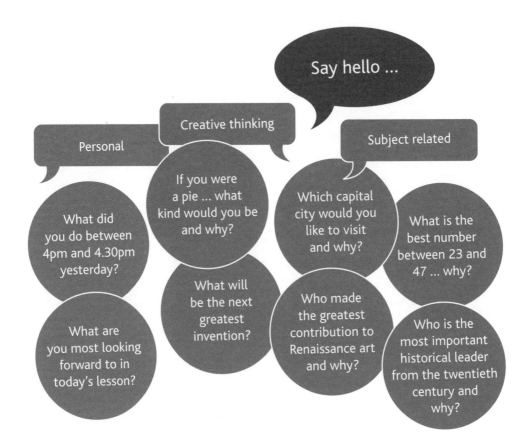

Learning sessions that start with an explicit 'Hello to (insert name)' as in the diagram above, given by everybody in the room, asserts that every learner belongs. This enables everyone to greet each other and hear their voice out loud from the start. At a deeper level, it affirms every learner as an individual member of the group and that each has an entitlement to be listened to and heard. This can be achieved by using a simple creative thinking starter prefixed with a simple 'Say hello' to the person sitting on their right, or a question like 'If you were the weather, what kind of weather would you be and why?' or 'If you were a number, what kind of number would you be and why?' Alternatively, you could ask the group to set each other a challenge, 'I challenge the whole group to achieve the toughest learning outcome by the end of today's lesson.'

The time invested in getting to know our students in a deliberate way, and working with them to develop their group values, is paid back in full when we see them accelerate their way through the curriculum. Learning in this way tends to happen with far fewer disruptions and behavioural issues because students are in an emotionally secure learning environment. It makes sense that we should treat each other, learners and colleagues, in a personal way. And it should feel fairly uncomfortable if we say we can't do this because we don't have time. Teachers who put emotional awareness at the heart of their learning design would argue that we don't have the time *not* to.

We have known for some time that emotional intelligence is as important, and some would argue more important, than intellectual intelligence. An emotionally aware classroom isn't simply one where we gently encourage everybody to be kind to each other. Clearly this is important, but we'd be missing a huge opportunity if we limited our emotional learning design to developing a set of ground rules at the beginning of term and only revisiting them when things get difficult.

Designing learning opportunities with emotional learning at the core will result in the creation of truly powerful learning opportunities that make an indelible tag in the memory banks of every learner. Ask anyone to recall their most memorable learning experiences and the chances are they will include many of the statements you'll see on the following pages.

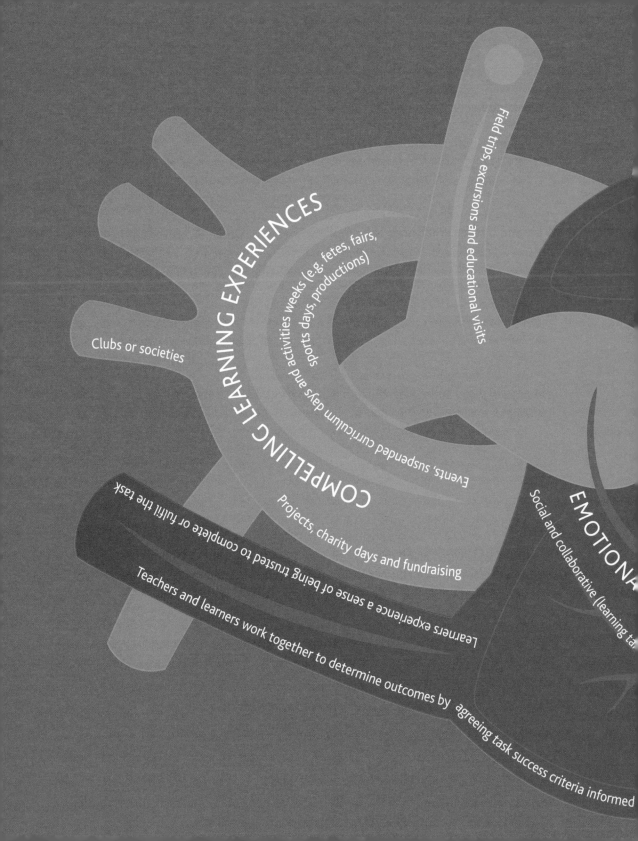

COMPELLING LEARNING EXPERIENCES

Field trips, excursions and educational visits

Clubs or societies

Events, suspended curriculum days and activities weeks (e.g. fetes, fairs, sports days, productions)

Projects, charity days and fundraising

Learners experience a sense of being trusted to complete or fulfil the task

Teachers and learners work together to determine outcomes by agreeing task success criteria informed

EMOTIONA

Social and collaborative (learning ta

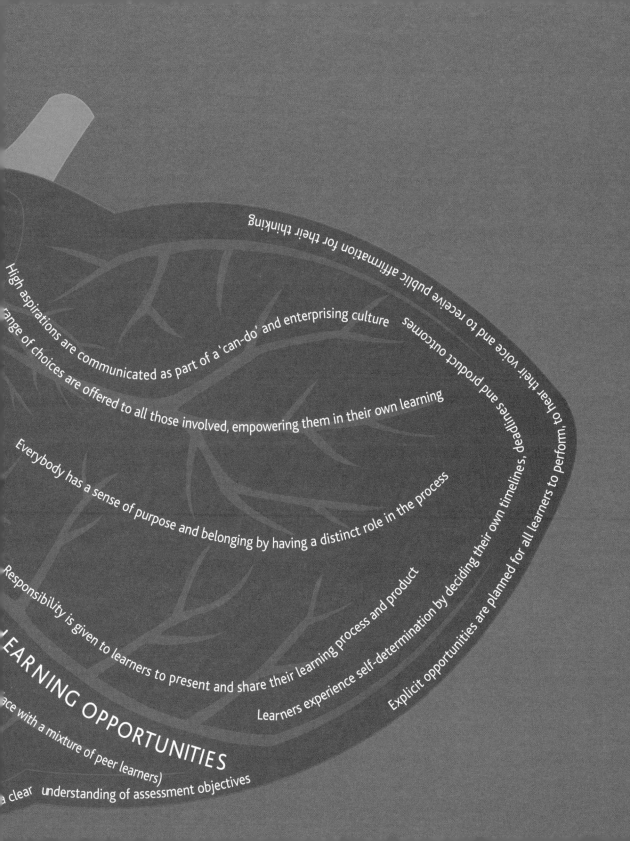

to hear their voice and to receive public affirmation for their thinking

High aspirations are communicated as part of a 'can-do' and enterprising culture

deadlines and product outcomes

range of choices are offered to all those involved, empowering them in their own learning

Everybody has a sense of purpose and belonging by having a distinct role in the process

to hear their voice and to receive public affirmation for their thinking

Responsibility is given to learners to present and share their learning process and product

Learners experience self-determination by deciding their own timelines, to perform,

Explicit opportunities are planned for all learners to perform,

LEARNING OPPORTUNITIES

ace with a mixture of peer learners)

a clear understanding of assessment objectives

The trick is to recognise the characteristics of these compelling learning experiences and integrate a rich mixture of them into the learning we provide as a part of the daily curriculum diet. In this way, we can design specific learning opportunities that provide:

 A safe environment for learners to feel confident to make contributions

 The active promotion of intellectual risk-taking, encouraging speculation, guessing, hypothesising and just having a go

 The encouragement for learners to challenge themselves and each other without fear of failure, ridicule or embarrassment

Emotional learning architecture

During the early stages of designing a new building, an architect will ask fundamental questions that have very little to do with materials, measurements or even function. In fact, they may not ask questions about the building as a physical construction at all at this stage. Instead, they ask questions about the 'space' they are creating:

How do we want people to *feel* when they use this space?

What will enhance people's *personal experience* and understanding of this space?

How will we ensure this space gives *memorable, compelling and enjoyable* experiences for those who use it?

How will we enable this space *to add something of value* to the people who use it?

How will we *make this experience tangible* for everybody who experiences it?

If we ask these sorts of questions of lessons that we design, we're well on the way to deliberately meeting the emotional learning needs of our learners. In doing so, we get to address the emotional age of the learner, make the learning relevant and meaningful for them and, most of all, make it clear that it is a safe enough place to take some intellectual risks. Being aware of the emotional response we want to try to provoke in lessons allows us to find ways to prompt *positive* responses deliberately and avoid *negative* emotional tags. You only have to look at the way many successful advertising campaigns are structured. They all seek to provoke an emotional response to their product to make it memorable to consumers. In this case, 'memorable' means funny, quirky, unexpected, unusual, distinct, silly and so on. So how about borrowing from the accumulated knowledge of market research to tweak your lessons so they too speak to the emotional brains of your learners? This is not to say that every lesson needs to contain *all* of these elements, but to design lessons without *any* appeal to the emotions of your learners is definitely a missed opportunity.

If we deliberately design learning that addresses emotion right from the outset, then we'll get to the heart of what powerful learning is all about. The content will naturally wrap itself around the emotional space you have designed. So, when we create learning opportunities, we can consider the emotional triggers in the table on pages 62-66.

Full On Learning Emotions:

Happy, elated, curious, safe, energised, belonging, interested, engaged, purposeful, meaningful, relevant, intrigued, self-esteem, worth, reflective, self-belief, connected, coherent, eager, anticipatory, courageous, empowered, valued, self-directed, in-control, self-aware, excited

LEARNING DESIGN QUESTION	PRACTICAL STRATEGIES	EMOTIONAL TRIGGERS, PROMPTS AND RATIONALE
What will enhance learners' *personal* experience and *personal* understanding of this learning opportunity?	Explicitly invest time to establishing a learning community using a 'check-in' that makes sure that everybody gets to hear their voice out loud within the first five minutes of the lesson	This makes it safe to try, to guess and to fail or succeed in equal measure. It personally welcomes every try, suggestion and attempt with openness by insisting that learners' names are used by the whole class
	Provide unusual, unfamiliar and unexpected visual stimuli, clues, artefacts and/or props to illustrate key learning points. Bring in something from your own experience, history or use the virtual world to introduce the unfamiliar	This puts everybody on a level playing field by using objects and stimuli that nobody has encountered. Everybody can have a guess about what, why and how the object is used. This provokes excitement, stimulates interest and enhances engagement
	Present ideas, processes, concepts and tasks with storytelling and strong narrative. Use storybooks, e-books, graphic novels with few words or explanations, leaving the learners to discover their own meanings and make their own connections	This enables learners to make individual meaning through their personal responses. Interpretations can be developed through a non-threatening, authentic, open and enquiry-based approach, rich with questions and personal areas of curiosity
	Present original sources, archives and/or real situations or problems from history, current affairs or external visitors	This generates intrigue and interest in what is new, unfamiliar, real and pertinent. It broadens learners' sphere of experience and extends their worldview beyond their immediate environment and culture

How will I ensure that this learning is *personally* memorable, compelling and satisfying?

Set in real-life contexts. Give authentic challenges with real meaning and genuine consequences to promote a sense of 'can-do' and high learning aspirations	This provides an explicit rationale for learning by presenting a clear connection to the relevance and purpose of what the session is about. By making the why of learning clear from the outset, learners are secure in knowing both what and why it is being asked of them
Present ideas and concepts in different, sense-rich and stimulating ways. Use infographics, diagrams, music and audio to enhance the information being presented and stimulate memory triggers	This deliberately prompts curiosity by asking learners to respond to and employ new and unfamiliar ways of presenting information. Visual and audio hooks can be used to trigger emotional responses and create positive memory tags for learning
Stagger the revelation of key information at planned moments during the session, rather than show it all at once at the beginning or saving it until the end	This builds and maintains a strong sense of anticipation, curiosity and intrigue. By using clues, puzzles and mysteries you can deliberately promote a sense of independent discovery for learners
Change the physical learning space, from moving the desks around, changing the wall displays, to redecorating the classroom or moving to a different place entirely	This can provoke a whole range of positive physical–emotional tags to enhance learning memories and prompt new reactions to learning
Invite visitors as 'experts', other colleagues or external guests to fulfil a specific role within the lesson, either physically or virtually. Ask them to present, operate a help-desk, facilitate, team-teach or observe the learning and provide feedback	This actively encourages social learning opportunities by encouraging learners to work with different people and create new social learning tags

Full On Learning Emotions:

Happy, elated, curious, safe, energised, belonging, interested, engaged, purposeful, meaningful, relevant, intrigued, self-esteem, worth, reflective, self-belief, connected, coherent, eager, anticipatory, courageous, empowered, valued, self-directed, in-control, self-aware, excited

LEARNING DESIGN QUESTION	PRACTICAL STRATEGIES	EMOTIONAL TRIGGERS, PROMPTS AND RATIONALE
	Offer learning choices and autonomy in specific areas – time to complete the task, who to work with, the specific areas upon which to focus or how they wish to present their final learning product	This provides learners with a sense of empowerment, self-direction and self-efficacy by enabling them to plan what choices they can make as they lead their own learning
	Use new learning tools, ways of presenting ideas or technology. Encourage cross-curricular learning styles, e.g. maths–art, music–science, philosophy–French	This enhances engagement and promotes a sense of excitement by varying the array of learning tools available. Expert learners in different subject areas can find a way to lead learning in a new subject area
	Organise groups in unfamiliar ways, using different pairings to expose learners to alternative viewpoints and to develop social learning skills	This taps into the social learning memory to act as a powerful emotional tag to aid cognitive memory

How will I know that this learning opportunity adds real *personal* value to every learner?		
	Structure and implement mini-plenaries to seek feedback throughout	This uses best practice from coaching strategies to encourage a culture of reflection and promote a sense of self-worth
	Use a feedback wall, mini-whiteboards or sticky notes. Make sure you provide feedback for every learner by name	By amplifying the voice of every learner you can promote an authentic sense of belonging
	Gather before/after sticky notes	Knowing and seeing that a learning change has happened enhances self-awareness and a sense of achievement. This, in turn, promotes a 'can-do' attitude to all learning
	Use the 'challenge target' for self- and peer-assessment	This results in all learners feeling a sense of self-direction and power over their personal learning journey
	Document the learning with photographs, notes, film and/or audio	The learning progress made visible and tangible will promote an individual and personal sense of achievement

Full On Learning Emotions:

Happy, elated, curious, safe, energised, belonging, interested, engaged, purposeful, meaningful, relevant, intrigued, self-esteem, worth, reflective, self-belief, connected, coherent, eager, anticipatory, courageous, empowered, valued, self-directed, in-control, self-aware, excited

LEARNING DESIGN QUESTION	PRACTICAL STRATEGIES	EMOTIONAL TRIGGERS, PROMPTS AND RATIONALE
What will I do to make this compelling learning (progress) explicit for every learner?	Integrate regular opportunities for learners to articulate their thinking and learning	This encourages a strong sense of self-awareness through explicitly offering opportunities for reflection, self-analysis and goal-setting
	Lead a debriefing session with unpacking meta-learning questions. Integrate this into the beginning of the next learning session	This promotes personal responsibility for the development of learning skills alongside cognitive development. This, in turn, promotes a sense of individual achievement and sense of progression for every learner
	Provide discrete opportunities for learners to present their learning to their peers and others at different stages of the learning process	Planned opportunities for the public affirmation of learning achievements will promote a sense of personal self-worth and enhances self-esteem
	Plan targeted feedback sessions with individual learners	Individualised and personal learning opportunities will promote confidence and the learners' energy and courage to learn more

Action Research

How can I establish a safe learning community for all learners?

How can I quickly develop positive relationships between myself and learners, and learners and their peers?

How can I provide regular opportunities for every learner to hear their voice out loud?

How can I encourage learners to listen to each other and gain a sense of belonging to this learning group?

How can I get even the most reticent learner to share their ideas and thinking with me and their peers?

How can I address and respond to inaccuracies in thinking in a safe learning culture?

How can I ensure feedback on learning is a two-way process that informs my planning?

What does risk-taking really look, sound and feel like for me and my learners?

How do I recognise risk-taking in my own educational practice?

When it happens, what do I consciously need to do to ensure it becomes characteristic of the learning that I promote?

Learning

To + '8

of

Process

e % - as +

89

product

LEARNERS WHO ...	TEACHING THAT ...
Are self-aware, reflective and actively seek to develop their skills and expertise	Enables all learning to be subjected to peer scrutiny to develop learners' intellectual resilience
	Focus: Peer-assessment
Use focused feedback from teachers and peers to develop their own expertise	Encourages quality learning conversations, developing a reflection-centred classroom with an explicit focus on learning
	Focus: Feedback

DEVELOPING EXPERTISE

It's all about learning

Learning cuts across every domain of human experience and interaction, from business, education, music, technology, entertainment, to gardening and sport. Bookshops and magazines are full of books and articles that focus on the holy grail of 'How to succeed in ...', laying bare the stories and working processes of successful people from all walks of life. There is a market for these publications because we *all* want to learn how to be better at what we do. We constantly seek to improve and develop mastery in whatever has piqued our interest, be it cooking, playing the guitar, developing our career or learning Pilates.

The world is rich with ideas and insight which the expert learner constantly seeks out and harvests to feed their personal world of learning. They know what excellence looks like and they seek to replicate it. They are greedy for ideas and insight. They are relentless in their search for new knowledge and understanding. They are inventive in their application of skills and concepts. They are addicted to learning.

Developing a learning addiction

As soon as she retired, after an exhausting 30-year career in teaching, my mother-in-law signed up to art classes with the 100 per cent commitment of a perfect student. The work she has since produced is really good and is proudly displayed around her home. She loves her art classes and is utterly dedicated to developing her technique, trying out new media and learning more about her abilities. She is enthralled by the excitement and challenge of developing her expertise and aspires to experience her own level of mastery[14]. Her learning commitment is to herself, to her ability and to her passion. There is no external reward awaiting her, no Turner Prize around the corner. Instead, her motivation comes from knowing what she wants to achieve and finding - and then learning - ways to realise this.

What happens when we tap into the determination to get better at what we do is that we learn more about ourselves. Given the opportunity we often surprise ourselves that (a) we *can* do something and that (b) we *get better* at it the more we do it. In most instances, there is no financial gain in dedicating ourselves to such pursuits and often, no public acknowledgement for our endeavours. All we have is the pure and simple desire to improve and, with deliberate practice, we start to believe that we *can* improve. We know what 'good' looks – and feels – like and this feeds us with a powerful motivating force to keep at it. This urge is best described as an 'aspiration to mastery'. It is the life-force of our learning addiction. And this is just what we want our learners to discover as they develop their own learning expertise.

Mastery is exactly what our learners need to achieve both *in* and *through* their learning. They need to develop a deep self-awareness in the different domains in which they operate, whether specific subject areas, playground politics or full-scale presentations at open evenings.

---

14 Daniel Pink shares his ideas about motivation in a business context in an engaging animated talk he gave as part of the wonderful RSA Animate Series found here: http://comment.rsablogs.org.uk/videos/page/3/and there's more in his book, Pink D., *Drive: The Surprising Truth About What Motivates Us* (Canongate Books: Edinburgh, 2010).

The problem of the expert – for learners

In order to become accomplished at something it needs to become second nature to us. We need to do it without thinking about it. But this makes it difficult when it comes to explaining to somebody else exactly what it is we're doing that makes us so skilled. Think about any exceptional athlete, musician or artist in full flow. If you ask them what makes them good, they will often struggle to give specifics. In addition, their ability may be so exceptional that when we watch them in action we end up describing them as having 'natural' or 'inherent' talent. As such there is an implication that their exceptional ability has come about as a result of luck or genetics.

For learners to develop expertise in any given area, they need to know exactly what 'excellence' or 'quality' looks, sounds and feels like. And so do we. Although this seems fairly straightforward, there is an inherent challenge in identifying and articulating exactly what it is that makes us *really* good at something. This is what I refer to as the 'problem of the expert'.

This is important because of what we need to have in place in our classrooms explicitly to develop expertise. This includes:

1. Teachers actively and regularly acknowledging the *effort* invested by learners in developing their skill or understanding. This prevents them from assuming that X will always be '*that* good' and that it 'all comes easily' to him/her.

2. Knowing that the confidence of every learner is fuelled by effort-focused praise. They are open and ready to take intellectual risks because they know it is effort that will determine the outcome as opposed to some magical, unattainable stroke of good fortune.

3. Making sure that every effort is acknowledged – high attainment is not taken for granted or assumed. This keeps all learners true and honest in their endeavours. The whole group feels it is safe to aspire to excellence.

They know what quality looks, sounds and feels like and they know what they need to do to achieve it.

4 Ensuring there is no fear of 'failure' because the whole group learns together. Model answers become aspirational documents rather than unattainable examples of perfection. Steps to excellence are regularly discussed as part of a clear and deliberate routine of 'This is what quality looks like ...' and 'This is how it can be achieved ...'

The problem of the expert – for teachers

As teachers, we have developed high levels of expertise in our subject – but this is precisely where the problem of the expert really comes to the fore. To develop expertise, you are no doubt aware that we must move through the following stages:

1 Unconscious incompetence, 'I haven't got a clue what's going on here.'

2 Conscious incompetence, 'I know I'm not very good at this.'

3 Conscious competence, 'I know what I can do ... and what I need to do to improve.'

4 Unconscious competence, 'I can do this without really thinking about it.'

But, for teachers, there is an additional stage:

5 Intuitive competence, 'I can predict and adapt instantaneously to learners' needs'.

The problem of the expert

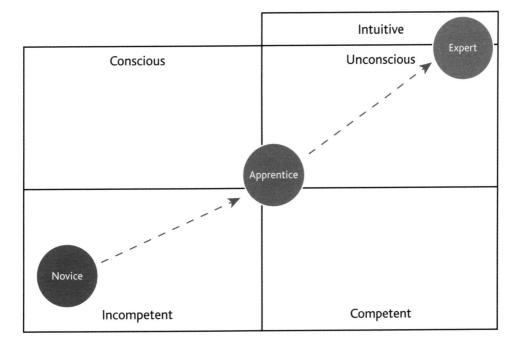

One of the defining characteristics of high levels of competence is that it becomes almost habitual. We can act 'without thinking' because the process, through practice, repetition and development, has become deeply embedded in how we think and act. And that's why teaching can be so difficult to unpick and work out what's really going on. It's incredibly difficult to pare-down expert practice to the nuts and bolts ready for somebody else to put it back together in their own way to achieve the same level of excellence. The same can be true when we are trying to explain effective learning to learners. To explain what has become natural to us and articulate our innate actions or thinking processes is a challenge for any expert in their field. However, when it comes to developing expertise in our learners, this is exactly what we must do. The journey towards expertise requires us to piece together elements of understanding that have become part of our own complex internalised network of knowledge that no longer requires conscious thought – intuitive competence. Voilà, the problem of the expert.

Furthermore, the problem of the expert can appear at any time. For some, it might be when we are supporting a learner who is struggling with a concept or skill that we mastered a long time ago. No matter how many times we explain it or demonstrate it, the learner just doesn't get it. It can just as easily appear when we are working with those learners who have grasped the basics and now need to push themselves to achieve very specific levels of expertise. It can then become an issue when we try to unpick *exactly* what it is about a skill or concept that they need to focus on and develop. This can often be particularly true for learners who have already achieved a good level of competence and understanding and who are ready to progress to another level. To make appropriate progress towards mastery and expertise involves *them* taking an intellectual - and inevitably an emotional - risk and for us to identify and articulate exactly what they need to aim for and how to achieve this.

There are five ways to develop expertise:

 **Identify quality learning.** Know what expertise looks like in any given area of learning. Regularly share the specific characteristics of 'quality learning' and excellence in the topic/subject/skill with your groups. For example: How does an excellent mathematician/historian/geographer/musician/physicist think and approach this problem/challenge? What does a quality answer look like? What does a quality team sound/look/feel like?

 **Remark on learning moments.** Identify and comment on the characteristics of excellence and quality as soon as you see them. Remark upon them in the context of the subject or skill being developed and actively acknowledge them, 'I like the way you did X to show that Y is the solution to ...' or 'The detail of X in your answer reflects a very secure knowledge and understanding of Y ...'

Share a language of learning. Ensure that *all* learners share an appropriate language of learning informed by the characteristics of expertise being developed. We can do this by talking and thinking about the subject or topic in terms of the specific language we want learners to develop. For example, in art, 'creative literacy', in music, 'musical literacy' or in history, 'historical literacy'. In this way, we can be really specific about the way in which we want learners to articulate their thinking in our lessons and they'll be able to start thinking and behaving like a scientist/geographer/mathematician. We can take this opportunity to explore any technical language and reinforce this by using it in our conversations with them and remark upon it when we hear it being used in learning conversations.

4   **Encourage conscious practice.** Design explicit opportunities for learners deliberately to practise the specific characteristics of effective learning in the subject. Talking through our learning as we are doing it is a useful way to practise this in a very conscious way. This can be supported by using specific learning outcomes and success criteria as anchors for regular plenaries to consolidate learning and encourage reflection. These become excellent markers for recognising and showing progress throughout the lesson.

5   **Plan for expertise development.** Integrate regular opportunities for learners to develop the characteristics of effective learning in every lesson and across a unit of learning. We can integrate these specific learning goals into the curriculum from the outset and use them as markers against which to evaluate progress when the unit is complete.

In developing our awareness about the specific characteristics of effective learning, we immediately become learners ourselves – a powerful and high impact way to model learning. We can then deconstruct the complex web of quality learning characteristics and unravel them. These can then be used as discrete learning goals.

Developing expertise with deliberate practice

The 10,000 hours theory been written about widely.[15] The thinking goes that to become the Bill Gates, Donald Bradman or Paula Radcliffe of our chosen field, we need to spend at least 10,000 hours practising, training and honing our skills. (When it comes to teaching expertise, 10,000 hours at 10 hours a day for 40 weeks a year translates to about five years – make of that what you will!)

The theory is helpful in underpinning the assertion that those who develop mastery have done so as a result of hard work and dedication, rather than natural talent. Admittedly, there may well have been a helpful dose of luck along the way – a natural disposition, body shape or cognitive ability – but the greatest influence on talent development is effort and a very deliberate kind of practice.

Teaching for expertise

We can design learning that will explicitly develop expertise by supporting deliberate, mindful practice. This equates to:

 Providing clear and specific identification of what an expert response looks, sounds and feels like in the area being explored.

 Placing ourselves in the role of observers of learning. In this way, we can recognise and celebrate the characteristics of expertise when they appear. These can then be reinforced through deeper learning opportunities to increase the challenge and consolidate learning.

---

15 Anders Ericsson first came up with the 10,000 hours theory. More recently, Daniel Coyle, Malcolm Gladwell and Carol Dweck have developed his thinking further. See Coyle, D., *The Talent Code: Greatness Isn't Born. It's Grown. Here's How* (New York: Bantam, 2009); Gladwell, M., *Outliers: The Story of Success* (New York: Little, Brown and Company, 2008); and Dweck, C. S., *Mindset: The New Psychology of Success* (New York: Random House, 2006).

3 Using an effort-focused language of learning. This results in praise being about effort and specific achievement.

4 Encouraging learners to take the lead and model and articulate the specific steps required to achieve expertise – making progress explicit throughout the lesson and enabling continuous on-going assessment.

5 Setting an aspirational, positive 'can-do' learning environment for all.

Expertise-focused learners:

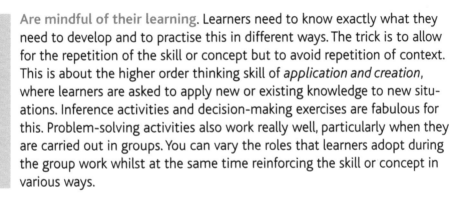

Are mindful of their learning. Learners need to know exactly what they need to develop and to practise this in different ways. The trick is to allow for the repetition of the skill or concept but to avoid repetition of context. This is about the higher order thinking skill of *application and creation*, where learners are asked to apply new or existing knowledge to new situations. Inference activities and decision-making exercises are fabulous for this. Problem-solving activities also work really well, particularly when they are carried out in groups. You can vary the roles that learners adopt during the group work whilst at the same time reinforcing the skill or concept in various ways.

Seek quality feedback. This is where our role as observer comes in. Once we have set up the learning, you can stand back, observe, seek and provide specific feedback in a number of ways. In fact, this 'stand-back' strategy is possibly one of the most powerful things we can do. There's more on it throughout this book. If we are really to ensure that learners make great progress and genuinely 'get it', we need actively to SEEK evidence that this has happened. The best way to do this is to observe the learning as it takes place. Do this and we've got continuous on-going assessment to inform our next steps. The power of the sticky note has already been mentioned, but it comes into its own when we want to give specific, immediate and non-intrusive feedback. Learners can then capture their own learning and have regular opportunities to reflect on this – articulating their thinking and expressing their understanding of where they are, where they need to be

and what they need to do to get there. Taking photographs during lessons and uploading them to play back during the activity or as part of a plenary works well to provide specific feedback. It also allows us to show progress in learning, reflecting this back to the learners as a document of the lesson. If we ask learners to do this for themselves – identifying key learning moments for themselves and each other – then all the better!

Respond to a purposeful context. Deliberate practice needs to be made as relevant to learner needs as possible and tasks need to be clearly linked to learning goals. Learners must see the point of why they are doing a task and how it connects with the subject and the real world wherever possible. Every subject can do wonders to make context really matter in learning – motivating learners to practise specific skills because they see the relevance of spending time and effort on their learning.

Action Research

How can I support learners to deliberately develop expertise?

How do I share the characteristics of 'quality learning' with all learners so that they know what to focus on?

How can I explicitly communicate high aspirations through the learning opportunities I design?

How can I ensure that effort is the focus of any praise?

What range of activities will encourage mindful practice?

What learning activities can I design to allow me to be an observer of learning and give specific feedback?

What are the component parts to the process of learning in this unit/topic/lesson?

How can I assess and show progress throughout a single lesson and over a unit of learning?

How can I develop a specific language of learning to support quality learning conversations in lessons?

What links can I make between specific learning goals and the wider context of the topic/subject?

How can I engender a culture of deliberate practice that is varied and engaging?

Creativ

is as important

and we should treat it with

ity...

in education as

literacy

the same
status

Sir Ken Robinson
'Why schools kill creativity' TED Talk 2006

LEARNERS WHO ...	TEACHING THAT ...
Engage their imagination, creative thinking and capacity to question new and existing scenarios	Explicitly develops creative thinking through divergent thinking strategies, open-ended questions and challenges

Focus: Creativity |
| Create new knowledge by making creative links between prior and present learning | Draws on existing knowledge to apply to new situations and contexts through problem-solving tasks and to make new links

Focus: Problem-solving challenges |

CREATIVE THINKING

All children start their school careers with sparkling imaginations, fertile minds, and a willingness to take risks with what they think.

Sir Ken Robinson[16]

If you've ever watched small children exploring their environment and encountering new objects, you will have observed them feel, taste, test out and generally apply a series of thoughtful tests to define where they are and what is around them. This process requires them to employ an open and exploratory approach involving speculation and high order thinking.

We are programmed to learn in this way. We construct our own understandings informed by our experience, environment and natural dispositions. Our very first learning strategy is play – or 'safe learning'. It is a no-pressure-try-something-new approach that leads to deep exploration and discovery. It also incorporates fun, excitement and imagination. If this is how we are predisposed to learn, then it makes sense to find ways to build these characteristics into the learning opportunities we design. Focusing on ways to foster creative thinking is a great place to start. It is what we all need to keep doing in order to keep learning.

The question of how to foster creativity and creative thinking in schools has been with us for a long time. In 1998 the National Advisory Committee on Creative and Cultural Education was formed to make policy recommendations to inform creative and cultural learning practice. The need for creative thinkers in all aspects of life has

16 *The Guardian*, Tuesday 10 February 2009

only intensified since their report *All Our Futures* was published. It provided a definition of creativity that has stood the test of time and has been quoted time and again by educational leaders, policy-makers and teachers:

'Imaginative activity fashioned so as to produce outcomes that are both original and of value.'[17]

The importance of creative thinking

As Albert Einstein asserted, 'We can't solve problems by using the same kind of thinking we used when we created them.' Along with an army of great minds over the centuries, there is now a critical momentum in recognising the importance of developing different ways of thinking as we move into the uncertain landscape of the future. Creative thinking needs to become the standard delivery vehicle of our curriculum, through the content it delivers. We need to ask learners to think creatively in maths, in science, in economics and well as be creative in drama, music, dance and art. Behaving creatively is one learning outcome we can't afford to ignore.

We recognise that the capacity to think differently, generate new possibilities and consider alternative approaches is vital in any effective learner and in all subjects. And the lovely thing is that we all have it in within us, from birth, to think and behave creatively. These attributes are the starting point for Full On Learning and they already exist in our students; they just need to be drawn out.

Some people assert that creativity, 'Happens like magic' and 'You've either got it or you haven't'. This assertion goes on to support the view that creative thinking cannot be taught. Full On Learning doesn't include an absolutist 'You've either got it or you haven't' view of *any* of our capacities. Don't get me wrong, some people *do* become more accomplished in their chosen areas of expertise and may have a

---

17 National Advisory Committee on Creative and Cultural Education, *All Our Futures: Creativity, Culture and Education* (London: NACCCE, 1999). Available at http://www.cypni.org.uk/downloads/alloutfutures.pdf (accessed 11 October 2011).

predisposition to working and thinking more effectively in a particular area. They may well have discovered their passion or made a connection with whatever it is that drives them. This is what Joseph Renzulli refers to as 'task commitment' and is a marvel to witness when we see it in action.[18] But we are all capable of more.

We all have the capacity for ...

Creative thinking, like any other kind of thinking, can be taught and developed by anyone. Bearing in mind what Picasso said about the human capacity for creativity – 'Every child is an artist. The problem is how to remain an artist once we grow up' – our ability to think and act creatively is clearly not the sole domain of some special group of extraordinary people. Whenever we encounter a new situation, we have to draw upon prior learning and experiences to make sense of the new context. That's creative thinking for you; we all do it and, more to the point, we are pretty good at it.

Why creative thinking?

Like all learning, effective learning is about instigating a personal change. Where there is change there is learning, and vice versa. Ideally, the change begins from the moment the learning session begins and, if it really works, will stay with learners beyond the classroom.

Learning that is deliberately designed to draw out the learner's capacity for creative thinking has a far greater chance of leaving a positive emotional tag on learning memories. Learning opportunities that rehearse creative thinking enable students

---

18 Renzulli, J. S., The Three-Ring Conception of Giftedness: A Developmental Model for Promoting Creative Productivity. In R. J. Sternberg and J. E. Davidson (eds), *Conceptions of Giftedness* (Cambridge: Cambridge University Press, 2005), pp. 53–92. Available at http://www.gifted.uconn.edu/sem/pdf/The_Three-Ring_Conception_of_Giftedness.pdf.

to build their confidence and resilience for open-ended tasks. None of us comes ready to deal with all the challenges that life will throw at us, but we are designed with the capacity to think creatively. We do need to practise though and creative thinking activities provide this opportunity. They're also good fun, and we tend to remember fun stuff with fondness.

Even if you don't believe that we are all born creative or have the capacity for creative problem-solving and thinking, creative thinking is far too important for us to leave to chance. We know that we can't just teach, hold our breath, cross our fingers and hope that learning will just happen, as if by magic.

Creative problem-solving

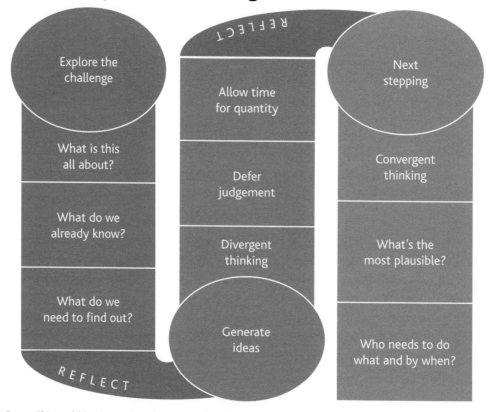

Source: This model has been adapted from a number of sources already around. For example: http://en.wikipedia.org/wiki/Creative_Problem_Solving_Process (correct as of April 2012).

If we accept that we *all* have the capacity to acquire and practise new skills and construct new understandings, it follows that we need to provide the opportunities and environment to make sure learning happens. Exactly *how* learning develops is clearly subject to a far more complex set of factors than simply being handed the opportunity, but presenting a well-designed learning scheme is a pretty good first step.

Step 1
Explore the challenge

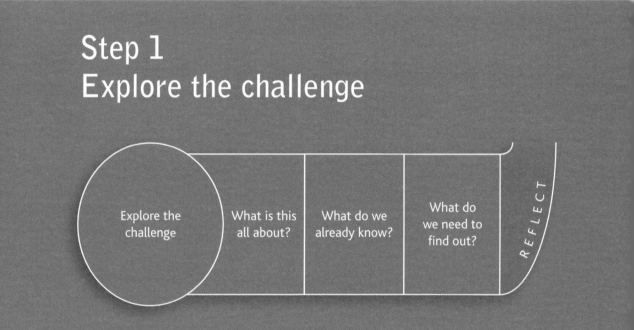

Let's take an example from, off the top of my head, 'Environmental Ethics'. The first step is for us to engage learners' imaginations. Admittedly, when faced with teaching environmental ethics to a group of surly teenagers, successfully engaging their imagination is no mean feat. But the power of imagination can bring to the fore all the elements of powerful learning (i.e. intrinsic motivation, engagement, excitement, inspiration) that can at times be so elusive. By considering how we might engage the imagination when we plan a topic, we can start to open up the possibilities of co-construction, choice and high order enquiry. When we do this, assessment questions may well change from:

Change from ...

What is the environment?

What do people think about the environment?

Why is the environment the topic of debate?

What is important about the environment?

To ...

What keeps me happy and healthy?

What is important to me? If I was fleeing from my country, what would I take with me and why?

What would I need to help me survive in a different habitat?

How would I adapt?

What would my chances for survival be?

After every step in the process, there needs to be a deliberately planned opportunity to reflect on how well the thinking process is going and to measure progress against the agreed success criteria. It also provides a vital connection or 'flow' between each *type* of thinking activity.

REFLECT

Step 2
Generate ideas

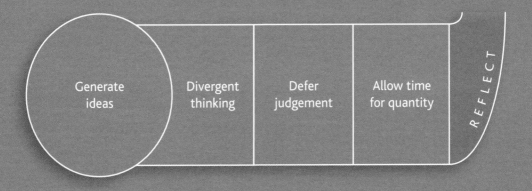

Using creative thinking starters not only engages learners from the outset but challenges them to begin the lesson using their brain rather more than may otherwise be the case. They require learners to make connections, draw on past experiences and make new meanings. The example below shows how a specific creative thinking activity works really well to actively engage the imagination for an environmental ethics topic. It is based on a joke – what do you call a penguin a the desert? – shared by my friend and colleague, Jim – The Lazy Teacher – Smith[19].

The first image uses a creative thinking starter (the answers provided are the most frequent responses in workshops). The second image takes the creative thinking (application of the imagination) into a specific context In this case, by using the context of a subject (geography in this instance), the creative thinking starter gives learners an open-ended, creative and *safe* way in which to explore the topic at hand. At the same time, it gives them an easy way to remember the learning conversations they have by giving them a personal connector (Gerald) to empathise with. By making Gerald the focus, the learners have something to make an emotional connection with, helping them to feel good, take a risk and have a go. All of

19 Smith, J., *The Lazy Teacher's Handbook* (Carmarthen: Crown House Publishing, 2010).

that in one activity: it provides the necessary structure for creative thinking to be applied to the topic whilst also providing an emotional safety net for those learners who find open-ended enquiry tasks daunting.

Step 3
Next Stepping

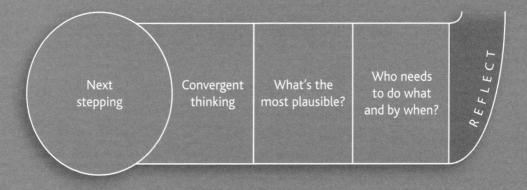

Many business thinkers refer to creative thinkers as 'right-brainers'.[20] As such they are accepting the neuroscience view that the human brain is divided into two: the creative stuff happens mainly in the right side of the brain and the logical stuff in the left.

When we are thinking creatively our brains get busy establishing new connections all over the place, between right- and left-brain domains, both in and between the emotional and the language-rich domains, between facts, experiences and senses. The brain pulls ideas apart and reconstructs the information in different ways and for different applications in new contexts. Once stimulated, the truly creative thinker is absorbed by the new connections being established between previously unconnected ideas, words and sounds. That's what creative thinking does.

One of my favourite activities that enables this type of thinking makes connections between previously unrelated concepts and ideas (useful for those tricky A-level 'synoptic papers').

---

20 Pink, D., *A Whole New Mind: Why Right-Brainers Will Rule the Future* (New York: Marshall Cavendish, 2008).

The 'Six Degrees of Separation' activity is designed to give learners an opportunity to very deliberately practise creative and connective thinking.

The activity can be can be developed and adapted in a multitude of ways:

You can add or reduce the degrees of connection

You can place very strict time limits on the activity to add a different kind of thinking pressure

You can insert your own topics/concepts/key words at any point

You can add your own 'stop-off' points in a longer list of degrees

You can use it as a starter or a revision exercise

You can use it to create groups in the class, asking students to link up with people with similar or different connections

And so it goes on. As with any form of good learning activity, you can squeeze out loads of value by using it in a variety of different ways and contexts. You should always demand a long shelf life from any activity or tool you invest time in developing.

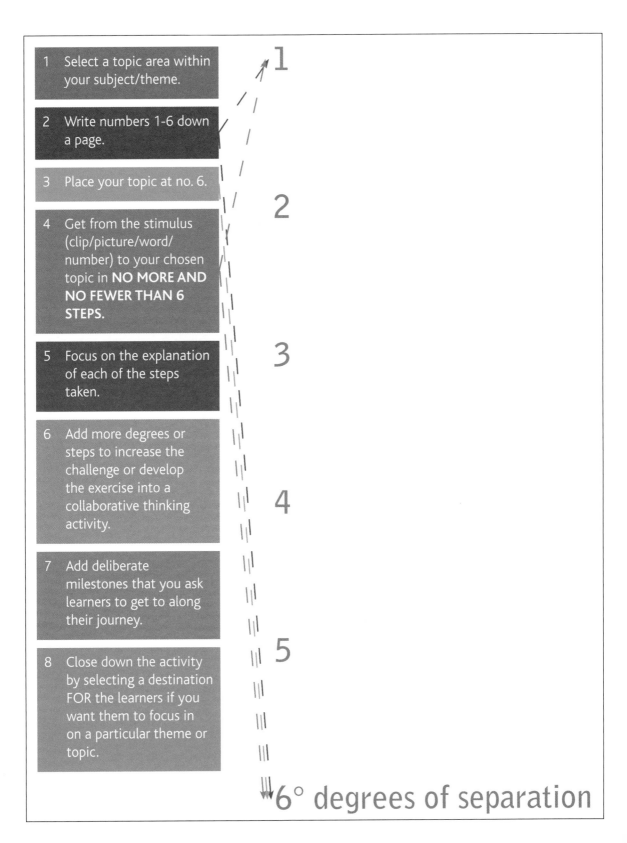

1 Select a topic area within your subject/theme.

2 Write numbers 1-6 down a page.

3 Place your topic at no. 6.

4 Get from the stimulus (clip/picture/word/number) to your chosen topic in **NO MORE AND NO FEWER THAN 6 STEPS.**

5 Focus on the explanation of each of the steps taken.

6 Add more degrees or steps to increase the challenge or develop the exercise into a collaborative thinking activity.

7 Add deliberate milestones that you ask learners to get to along their journey.

8 Close down the activity by selecting a destination FOR the learners if you want them to focus in on a particular theme or topic.

1

2

3

4

5

6° degrees of separation

Strictly creative thinking

The thing about creative thinking is that it requires rules. As such, it is not the terrifying 'anything goes' lesson that many teachers imagine. Creative thinking cannot happen unless there are some very strict boundaries in order to safeguard learners' intellectual welfare and, just as importantly, the quality and purposefulness of outcome.

In the six degrees of separation activity, the key is to enforce the rule of 'In no more or less than six steps'. This prevents learners rushing straight to the end. The whole point of the activity is to encourage a deliberate thinking journey that demands explanations of their thinking processes and makes use of a number of their personally selected connections. It only works if learners can provide a clear rationale, articulated to others, that explains every step along the way. There is also a good dose of autonomy as learners can select both 'destination' and 'stop-off' points. Using a random start point, the activity remains very open but if you want to close it down, simply choose the topic to start from or, alternatively, decide on the destination point. Closing the exercise down doesn't restrict creative thinking but it does provide another layer of intellectual safety for those learners who struggle with open-ended or divergent thinking tasks.

Here's another favourite activity which was inspired by a presentation I saw a few years ago given by Tim Brown, CEO of IDEO, an international design and innovation consultancy. The idea is simple: adapt as many of the 30 circles in whatever way you choose in one minute. If you unpack this, the activity is simply a divergent thinking task but the fundamental element is the time restriction you place on it. By doing this, you give something concrete to those learners who may be reluctant to have a go at purely open-ended tasks that have no clear sense of purpose at the outset.

Saying, 'It's okay, there are no right or wrong answers' significantly breaks established cultural learning rules. Many learners will find it liberating to be given a free rein, but for others who thrive on knowing there is a definite answer (and they are used to getting it right), this is far from reassuring. In fact, 'no right or wrong answer – just give it a go' is one of the most frightening things they can hear at school

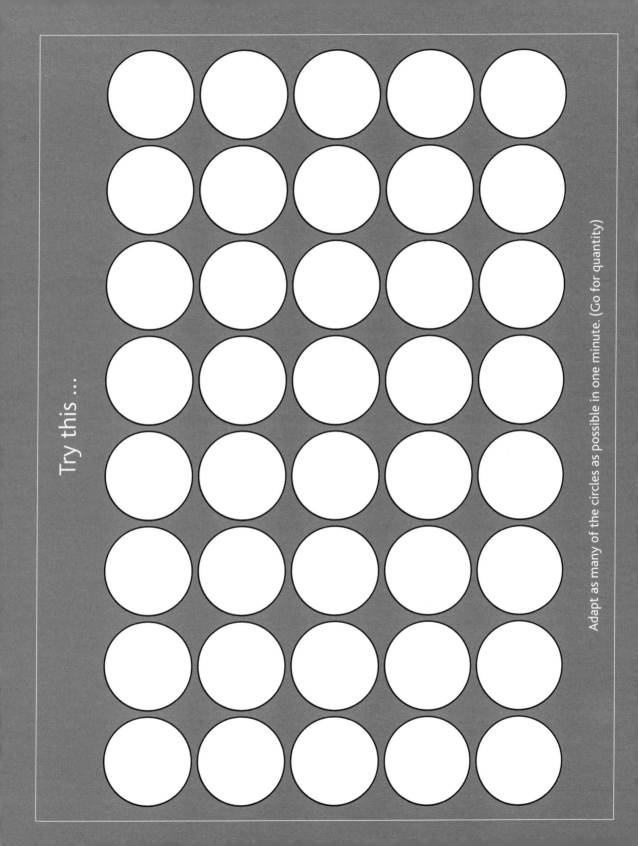

Try this ....

Adapt as many of the circles as possible in one minute. (Go for quantity) (see the creative risk gap on pages 102-103).Taking away the rules of any activity can be unsettling at best and threatening at worst. So, once again, we need to take account of the emotional brain first so that we ease learners into doing things differently. Regularly using these types of activity, supported by an effective debrief that focuses on the thinking process that learners go through, will help to quell any lurking resistance these learners might have to having a go.

Deepening thinking

One creative thinking activity that can help to developing learning resilience is the 'How would?' activity.

One example is the 'How would?' strategy, where we ask what a celebrity, animal or historical figure might think about a topic they have learned about or a solution that they have come up with. This is particularly good when we want to hear learners check out their thinking and reasoning. That way, we can assess the security of their understanding as they test-out what they have learnt in applying it to an unfamiliar context.

This activity also demands that learners hold one concept in their head whilst at the same time considering another more unusual idea (proper whole-brain thinking).

A valuable prompt you can give learners to help them to do this activity is to use 'whereas' or 'however' in their responses. Prompts like this act as useful 'tweaks' to encourage learners to compare, contrast and provide deeper responses.

If we are presented with an unfamiliar situation and are invited to play around with it using what we already know, we often find surprises when we apply the familiar to an unfamiliar situation. By doing this, we also get to check out our understanding of the familiar as we play with it in a new situation.

Hooks for creative thinking

The 'Would you rather?' activity exemplifies the way in which we can use entertaining material to lure learners into a comparative thinking exercise ahead of delving more deeply into a new topic. The fun element of the activity presents a non-threatening, low-risk entry point for all learners. No prior knowledge is required and there are clearly no right or wrong answers. From this point, you can introduce a topic-specific question based on the same principles of comparing two similar yet distinct objects or situations and asking learners to choose between them (e.g. two leading characters in a play, two bodily functions, two countries, two numbers, chemical compounds etc.). Just by tweaking the question stem, you can extract many lessons worth of discussion and debate in a way that deliberately engages the sense of humour and creates a positive emotional tag to learning.

By giving a physical 'voice' to the learning we want to encourage, we both validate it and celebrate it. If we display the process of learning alongside the products of learning, we send a message about what we want to see and what success looks like.

Our learners need to get used to dealing with new challenges on a daily basis. For the most part, they are pretty good at this. But one thing we can do very deliberately is to top up their reserves of learning resilience so they are able to cope with a new teacher, group, technology or difficult question. Providing a regular offering of creative thinking activities in our lessons will do just that.

For those who don't already have great reserves of learning resilience, a little intellectual security goes a long way to providing the impetus to try something different. Creative thinking provides learners with opportunities to rehearse a struggle and the chance to develop strategies that help get them through the hard bits. In doing so, they will be making connections for themselves, listening to alternative points of view and creating new knowledge with the benefit of others' thinking and expertise.

Resistance to new ways of thinking and learning

Creative thinking can easily fall prey to learning resistance. Whenever you hear learners ask, 'Why do we have to do it like this?' or 'What's this got to do with the exam?' you are may well be hearing, 'I feel really uncomfortable doing *anything* new or different as I can't guarantee the brilliance of the outcome. So let's do what I'm used to because I know I'm good at that.'

When it comes to creative thinking, it is critical that learners are sufficiently confident to fully embrace a 'try something new' approach. If they are to generate lots of ideas, they need to do so without being inhibited by self-censorship. To 'just try' sounds simple enough but it is probably the hardest thing, particularly when the outcome is not guaranteed to be good. For perfectionists and high achievers who feel that anything short of brilliance could, at any moment, completely destroy their painstakingly acquired reputation for high attainment, this lack of certainty can be enough to prevent them from trying *anything*.

For creative thinking to really flow through lessons, learning opportunities need gentle introductions that give learners the chance to familiarise themselves with different cultural learning norms. One way to provide emotional security is to involve them in the 'why', 'how' and 'what' of the lesson. By doing this, you can communicate why we are asking them to think and learn in this different way, how the lesson will be organised to make sure they get the most from it and what they are going to be learning. Another way to ensure that creative thinking is an exciting activity, and doesn't represent a threat, can be achieved by asking pupils to work collaboratively to create a response and generate ideas, rather than being left to come up with a single spark of inspiration all on their own.

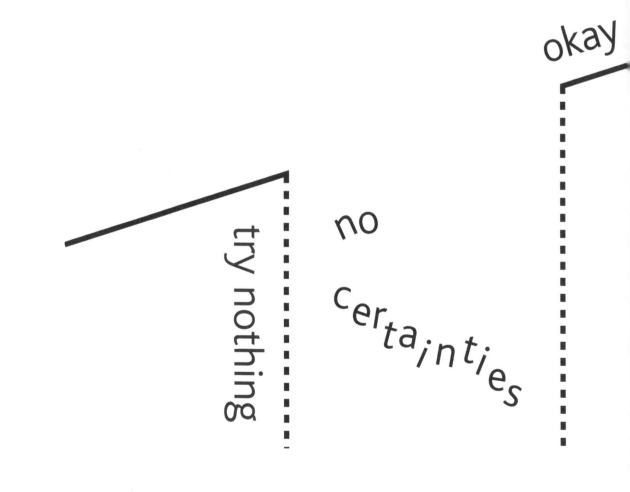

okay

no

certainties

try nothing

excellent

quality of outcome

try something

The creative risk gap

The 'why' of creative thinking

Those learners who have worked out which hoops to jump through to be identified as 'successful' (often those labelled as 'gifted and talented') are also often those most at risk of coasting and underachievement. Sometimes it is claimed that these learners respond positively to open-ended questions, often presented as having 'no right or wrong answers'. But this is not always true. Often they lack learning resilience when it comes to new intellectual and emotional challenges. It is worth noting that the reason why many of our most successful learners have reached their high levels of attainment is because they *know* for sure the 'right' answer. Take that away as a possibility for them and we are in danger of taking away the one thing about which they are guaranteed of success. In addition, when it comes to new and different ways of learning, they may be approaching these with far less resilience than other learners who have built up a repertoire of 'getting un-stuck' strategies. A rich, balanced diet with the essential nutrients of creative thinking will go a long way to addressing this issue.

We need to design frequent opportunities that deliberately develop innate learning capacities so that *all* learners become intellectually and emotionally resilient, can respond positively to challenge and comfortably inhabit the world of speculation and hypothesis. We need to draw out their capacity to explore new concepts and ideas and to develop new approaches to the world. Oh, and the same goes for *us* too.

Creative learners need creative teachers

We tend to teach in our preferred manner of learning. Therefore, if we define ourselves as 'not creative' it can feel more challenging to explicitly plan creative thinking activities into our lessons. The key to unlocking it is confidence. Just like our learners, we too must build the self-belief to try new approaches within our pedagogy. In doing so, we will find ourselves providing just the right conditions to draw out our learners' innate capacities to think creatively, generate ideas and be innovative.

Assessing creative thinking

When it comes to assessing creative thinking, instead of trying to capture elements of it and attaching levels, grades or scores, look instead at the *contribution* creative thinking has made to the learning process and outcome (i.e. how it has helped to meet the subject-specific criteria). Another trick is to observe the learning when it takes place and listen to how the language of learners reflects the characteristics of creative thinking.

I considered a number of alternatives before going with the final plan

We discussed our interpretations to the text and developed our ideas from this

We decided to present our project in different ways to reflect the personalities of the whole group

I adapted the ideas that I originally had before coming up with this solution

We weighed up the pros and cons before we made our final decision

Here are ten principles of creative thinking to incorporate into your lessons:

Making connections. In particular, between previously unrelated objects, facts, concepts and ideas. This means the brain is working very hard indeed! Learners should be able to articulate their thinking processes so you can assess the *quality* of the connections they make.

Time for exploration with others. Dedicated time and space needs to be planned so that learners can practise their creative thinking. Time also needs to be given to allow effective groups to form. Collaboration lies at the heart of quality creative thinking. It is a fundamental requirement in any creative thinking process that learners listen and respond to ideas and feedback from others. They need to be open to alternatives and prepared to change their mind. To allow this to happen, they have to feel safe.

Celebrate enjoyment. Creative thinking activities are inherently enjoyable. Learning objectives can reflect this by making 'fun' (which you can describe in your learning objectives as: be engaged, show your enjoyment, maintain your concentration, etc.) an explicit, intended outcome. Another way to think about creative thinking is that divergent thinking is the fun bit and convergent thinking is the purposeful bit, but that both are equally important for the quality creative thinking bit to take place.

Freedom within the rules. Creative thinking must be both contained and purposeful. Activities need to strike a balance between offering learners choices (i.e. what they will do, how they will do it, who they will do it with, when they need to do it by) whilst being clear about the purpose of the learning. Creative thinking can be a messy business, so lucid constraints mean that it will maintain purpose and direction. Constraints also ensure safety, particularly for those learners who lack intellectual and emotional resilience or find learning in new and unfamiliar ways threatening.

Creatively confident teachers. We all need to be ready for thinking in a creative way. As teachers we need to practise and develop *our* creative thinking alongside our learners. When was the last time you drew a picture? Tapped out a rhythm to a song in time with other group members? Played charades? Performed in front of others? We need to practise creative thinking activities for ourselves, to identify and reflect on our *own* responses to learning in different ways. In this way, we will be far more able to support those learners who find any new ways of learning threatening and/or pointless.

6   **Permission to try**. The creative risk gap is a barrier to many under-confident learners being able to try something new. The introduction of creative thinking activities can be gradual. Begin with a five-minute creative thinking starter (e.g. 'How many ideas can you come up with?') in response to a picture, piece of music, number or key word. Build from this into more extensive activities). In this way, you get to provide a low-stakes/high-engagement lesson.

7   **A balance between simplicity and complexity**. If there is too much information, this tends to close down thinking rather than encourage the brain to draw upon and create spin-off ideas and interpretations. For example, a half-picture of an egg will generate a far more creative and divergent discussion than a picture of a full egg box. In addition, the more information we give, the lower the challenge. And, as learners become more confident, you can increase the challenge by gradually reducing the amount of information you provide.

8   **Collaboration**. Truly creative insight rarely happens in isolated moments of inspiration; it thrives in company. We are naturally social beings and we love to spark off other people's ideas. We build, amend and adapt ideas and approaches with each other through articulating our thoughts and sharing these in groups. This is also true for practitioners: action research conducted in small groups within or between schools creates a fertile ground for innovative teaching and learning.

9   **Assess the language**. Listen for the contribution that thinking creatively has made to learning outcomes. By observing the learning, you can watch and listen to the learners as they think out loud and work things out together. Creativity is characterised by phrases like 'What if we tried ...?' or

'Has anybody got any other ideas?' or 'I was thinking it might be a bit like your idea but with some extra ...' and so on.

10 **Make learning visible.** Provide explicit opportunities for learners to publicly reflect on their learning with each other and back to you. This communicates to them that you value their creative thinking as an integral part of the process of learning alongside its end product. Leave time for groups to be able to present their work. This immediately creates fantastic opportunities for peer- and self-assessment and gives you a great way to demonstrate progress over any length of time.

Action Research

In what ways do longer-term projects promote creative thinking and confidence?

How do I support learners to independently generate their own ideas?

How do I assess creative learning behaviours?

How can I encourage learners to make creative connections between prior and present learning?

How can I support learners to consider, search for and apply a wide range of approaches?

What does progression look, sound and feel like in creative thinking?

What does creative thinking look and sound like?

How might giving choices to learners foster creative thinking?

What does my classroom say about the learning I want to see?

In what ways does the space encourage creative thinking?

How do learners *feel* when they are in my classroom? How do you know?

In what ways is it possible to make my classroom an engaging advertisement for my subject and how students learn within it?

If I value students' creativity, how is this apparent in the physical space in which they learn?

If I expect them to practise collaboration, autonomy and self-directed learning, what is available to them in the room to enable this to happen (resources, equipment, posters, visual clues and questions)?

If I want students to value the process of creative thinking over the product, how is this reflected in the wall displays? Who has work on the walls (is it finished, draft, thinking maps) ? What criteria for the displays of learning do I use? How is this agreed with students? Who is responsible for the room?

How does my learning environment 'scream' creative thinking?

the ˈme-shaped; space in the universe

LEARNERS WHO ...	TEACHING THAT ...
Know what they need to do so they can move from where they are now to where they want to be in the future	Makes frequent and appropriate use of curricular targets, assessing pupils' progress and explicit learning dispositions so learners are clear about what they need to do to progress. Encourages learners to take responsibility for their learning
	Focus: Triple whammy questions and competency-based curriculum
Know exactly what their role as a learner entails and are prepared to take it on	Regularly involves learners in the co-construction of the curriculum, learning intentions and success criteria

FIVE FULL ON
INVOLVEMENT

As I was embarking on my teaching career, I remember the emotionally charged session before the allocation of teaching practice schools. My fabulous PGCE tutor was asked by one of my slightly ashen-faced peers, 'Erm ... what would you say is the most important thing I need to do once I know my teaching practice school?' My tutor looked him straight in the eye, took a deep breath of resignation and after a momentary pause, simply replied, 'Plan. Plan as if it is a campaign of battle.'

To be honest, I think we were all hoping she would say something reassuring and practical like, 'Get a map, find out where your school is' or 'Find out where your classroom is and get the names of your students,' but this advice was actually far more valuable – in the long term at least. I'm pretty sure we all managed to find the right school on our own, but the planning? Well, therein lies a steep learning curve.

I've never forgotten my tutor's sage (if a little sinister) advice. Pointless knowing where the school is if, when you get there, you don't know why you're there, what you're going to do or how you're going to do it. The same is true for our learners. It is hard for them to get really involved and engaged in anything if they just don't see the point as I have mentioned earlier.

We know that when we plan our lessons, programmes of study and schemes of learning with sharpness, we are freed up to teach. It's like front-loading all our thinking, energy and activity so that when our great learning plan is laid at the feet of our learners, we can stand back and watch them rise to the challenges we have constructed – or even better, ask them to get involved in the thinking and planning with us. In other words, we are free to watch, listen and coach. We can then make very calculated and deliberate interventions to ensure that the fragile potential of every one of our learners is teased out.

Planning is thinking

We need to be clear about what we want learners to do, how we will direct them to achieve this and what actions we will make along the way to ensure that *every* moment is a learning moment. Our planning provides an infrastructure upon which learning can be built. It allows us to define exactly what we want learners to gain from being in our teaching care. It forces us to consider what learners need to know, do and be like *as a result of this* lesson. The quality of our design will make the difference between a lesson that simply fills the time and one that offers a truly compelling and worthwhile experience for everybody involved.

Unpack your learning expertise

Sir Ken Robinson, in his second TED Talk in 2010, presents a fantastic argument for the need not to just reform education, but to revolutionise it.[21] In it he reads an excerpt from Abraham Lincoln's speech to the second annual meeting of Congress in December 1862:

> The dogmas of the quiet past, are inadequate to the stormy present. The occasion is piled high with difficulty, and we must rise – with the occasion. As our case is new, so we must think anew, and act anew. We must disenthrall ourselves, and then we shall save our country.[22]

The way in which he unpicks the word 'disenthrall' in his talk is worth noting. He describes the way in which we need to un-couple ourselves from that which we take for granted in order to change and design things anew.

As teachers, 'disenthrallment' is an everyday act. We have all reached an incredibly high level of competence when it comes to learning. We are holders of at least one

---

21 Robinson, K., Bring on the Learning Revolution! (May 2010). Available at http://www.ted.com/talks/lang/eng/sir_ken_robinson_bring_on_the_revolution.html.

22 Available at http://showcase.netins.net/web/creative/lincoln/speeches/congress.htm.

degree and some kind of post-graduate qualification. We are by definition very practised and successful learners. Learning has become so ingrained in us that it is exceptionally difficult to identify, analyse and explain to others. But this is exactly what we must do. We must 'disenthrall' ourselves from our own intuitive learning competence and chunk it down for our learners to get really involved in developing their learning expertise.

One of the reasons why so-called 'non-specialist' teachers often become the most effective leaders of learning is because they are actively involved in their own learning. They are operating at the point, not of *intuitive* competence that I mention earlier, but of *conscious* competence, often teaching themselves in preparation to teach their groups.

The 'Triple Whammy' planning question

When developing gifted and talented policies, unpicking expertise is the most helpful place to begin. If we are able to recognise what it is that characterises 'high ability' in a particular subject area, we are far more likely to spot it and celebrate it when it occurs in learners, and thereby plan for it in the learning opportunities we design.

That is not to say that we can control all aspects of learning. The skill and craft of the teacher is to design learning so that specific skills can be acquired and knowledge constructed, whilst still leaving space for surprises. We are well-practised at identifying the knowledge or content component of lesson design. The learning skills that learners will need to deepen their understanding are similarly important to include in our learning design, however they often lurk in the realms of the intuitive. But there is a third element present in this magical concoction of learning which very often goes by unnoticed and left to chance – disposition.

When I think about 'dispositions' of learners, I think about them in terms of the readiness or openness of learners to learn. We all know that the ability of somebody to learn incorporates a powerful mix of emotions, skills, aptitudes and knowledge, based on what they already know and understand and what they can already do. Whether they are *ready,* and therefore *able*, to acquire more knowledge and understanding in a new, more challenging context and apply their skills to a new situation will often (although not exclusively) be informed by their learning dispositions. And these need to be developed through *conscious* practice.

I recently worked alongside a usually engaged, positive 12-year-old boy who had seemingly undergone a character-transplant in the space of one maths lesson. Having reached a certain point of competence with expanding and removing brackets, he had hit his own personal learning wall and come to a tearfully angry standstill. There was nothing wrong with his knowledge, understanding or the skills he had acquired to this point, but as the algebraic expressions had become more complex and the challenge increased, he didn't have (at that point) the tenacity and resilience to continue. Hence he met the wall.

So in order to get started again, all we did was to take a step back and *reflect* on the problems he had solved up to the point of his 'wall'. We highlighted one of the earlier problems that had been more of a struggle and *analysed* why he had found it difficult and how he had overcome this. He then *made a connection* to this and the 'wall' problem. With that, he was off again and, although he took longer, he got there in the end. Afterwards, we talked about what had happened and what he needed to 'be like' in order to overcome this particular learning wall:

'I just needed not to panic' (be calm, be objective)

'and to remind myself that I could do it' (be reflective, be positive)

'I also needed to not let it beat me' (be resilient and determined)

This then turned into a personal list of 'What I need to *be like* when I have to climb my learning walls in maths'. He wrote it in his student planner and can refer to it now whenever he finds something a struggle. Although we connected it to maths, it is equally applicable to any time he encounters a new learning wall.

It would be great if in his next maths lesson, his teacher asks the group to feedback, 'Who had difficulties with this task?' and 'What did you do to overcome your difficulties?' and that this then informed a quick discussion in response to:

'So what do we now know about what we need to *be like* to be great mathematicians?'

The responses could be used to inform future learning so that deliberate opportunities are designed to enable the group to practise and develop their levels of resilience and determination. This wouldn't change the content to be covered in the lesson, just the way in which it could be accessed.

I have seen some great work in schools that have created 'getting un-stuck' walls on their rooms. Learners *and* teachers share their own 'getting un-stuck' strategies on the classroom wall so that whenever a student finds something difficult, they can have a look for some ideas as to what they could do next, without always relying on the teacher to help them. These kinds of approaches are all about developing resilience, tenacity, determination, as well as encouraging learners to take responsibility for learning and fostering independence. Other ways to approach this are to create posters, bookmarks and publish in planners with a list of helpful strategies that learners can refer to. Creating a question-bank of questions that prompt resilience-fostering thinking is another way of doing this. There's a section on 'getting un-stuck' (resilience-fostering) questions in the chapter on questioning.

Dispositions: knowing what to look for

Here's an example of how just one disposition, *curiosity*, could be un-packed to inform the design of a lesson that aims to deliberately foster curiosity. By considering what a learner looks, sounds and feels like when they are *being* curious, this can help when we want to design a lesson to allow that to show. In addition, we then have a portrait of a curious learner that we (and the learners themselves) can specifically look out for during the lesson.

The characteristics of curiosity that we identify can become our key indicators that can be used to let the whole group know if they're on-track. We can then use the indicators as the specific language of learning for our feedback during regular progress-checks throughout the lesson. If you adopt the observing learning approach covered in this book, you can also write on sticky notes (or similar alternatives) to unobtrusively let learners know that you've 'caught' them being curious and to generate more questions to increase the flow of learning:

'That was a really great question, Billy, thank you.'

'You've asked four really great questions already, what's your next one?'

'You responded really positively to Sian's question. Now see if you can pose one of your own.'

'How will you find out more about what Jarred just said? Who could you ask? Where could you look? Who could you team up with?'

'How could you use what you are learning about in History to help you with this today?'

Designing a generic pen portrait for a 'successful' learner in a particular subject or topic is a way to build a series of indicators for what exactly *we* are looking for as they develop their expertise in a subject or topic. It also informs us as to exactly how we will design opportunities so that these qualities can show themselves. During lessons, we can look for the characteristics explicitly and grab every opportunity to let learners know exactly what we're looking for. This means we can give really specific feedback when we see these positive learning dispositions in full flow. So just as we need to be specific when we are looking out for and giving feedback on the knowledge, understanding and skills developed during the lesson, we can do it for dispositions in exactly the same way.

DISPOSITION

Focus on curiosity

LEARNING DESIGN

Phrase outcomes and objectives as questions

Open with a controversial statement or stimulus

Plan through questions

Regularly invite learners to 'Make their 'best guess' and work with them to find out how 'good' their guess is.

Regularly ask learners to feedback on their levels of desire to find out more confidence/excitement (thumbs up/traffic lights/RAG rate/continuum lines etc.)

Encourage hands-on exploration, investigation and play where it is possible – a conversion of 'What's your best guess?' into your 'What's your best try?'

Plan specific times to ask learners to reflect on what happened, what would have been better etc.?

Flip the topic, begin with the answer first. Invite learners to generate their own questions.

Ask learners to co-construct the success criteria and encourage speculation through 'What if?' 'What comes next?' 'What will happen if?' questions, present unusual objects linked to the topic and construct enquiry them, build sequences of questions, only answer a question with a question, 'What do you think?' 'What could you do next?' 'Who else could you ask?'

WHAT YOU ARE LOOKING FOR

Are learners asking 'good' questions?

Are they questioning each others' responses?

In what ways is the lesson characterised by questions?

What type of questions are there (high order; open; learning-focused etc.)?

Is everybody asking questions?

How do learners respond to new concepts, activities or situations?

Do learners want to find out more?

When do learners ask how this is related to other aspects of the topic/subject?

How are learners able to identify and list any new 'discoveries'?

How well do learners articulate their thinking processes?

How do learners construct their next steps?

What levels of confidence do learners display?

In what ways do learners direct their own learning?

Dispositions at the heart of a shared learning language

We can use the language of dispositions to develop a *shared* language of learning with learners so that the question,

'What do we need to *be like* in order to complete/succeed in this *task*?'

This a fantastic opportunity for a quality learning conversation. Often, this type of conversation is used to agree behavioural and conduct ground rules for the lesson. But to use it to its fullest extent you can take it even further and incorporate it into the success criteria for the product *and* the process of the learning, hand-in-hand.

Peer-assessment activities provide yet another opportunity to be explicit about the dispositions needed to be successful in a topic or subject area. When we ask learners to peer-assess each other's efforts, they can be asked to evaluate:

 How well they have *met the assessment criteria (Knowledge; Understanding and Skills)*

 The *way* in which they did it *(Dispositions: co-defined by the group and taking into account individual and general characteristics)*

You will know if you have ever been involved in a conversation like, '*creativity*; what *is* it anyway?' or, 'What exactly do we mean by *independent* learning?' the discussion that follows can become pretty subjective. For example, when I'm at my most creative (sociable soul that I am), I'm probably sitting on my own, isolated from any distractions with my headphones on. I'm quiet and completely shut-off from anything or anybody around me. On the other hand, for one of my colleagues, creative thinking for her is all about talking, big flip chart paper and involves at least two other people, preferably more. For some of our learners, it could be daydreaming, doodling, staring out of the window and *appearing* completely disengaged. (Worth a thought.)

So by asking learners to reflect on their *own* learning behaviours and what *we*, as teachers should be on the lookout for, we get to prompt a very personal take from the learners' point of view on, 'What successful learning looks like *for me*, when I'm doing it'. This directly involves them at the heart of our learning design. It also provides a great opportunity for us to ensure that what we are talking about when we ask them to 'think creatively' is the same thing that they understand as 'thinking creatively'. We can then be reassured that we have an agreed, shared and fully checked-out language for learning. And because *any* conversation that promotes self-knowledge can only serve to drive learning forward, it's a conversation well-worth having.

A while back I was introduced to what a friend of mine called the 'Triple Whammy Planning Question'; this allows us to consider all aspects of learning, including this magical 'disposition'.

First, within a particular subject area or topic, consider:

 What do learners need to know and understand as a result of this lesson/ subject/topic? (*knowledge and understanding*)

What do learners need to be able to do? (*skills*)

What do learners need to be like? (*dispositions*)

As adults and as teachers, we have achieved a high degree of mastery and can fairly easily identify the knowledge and understanding that we want learners to develop. Often, we find that the acquisition of skills happens as an integral part of acquiring the knowledge and understanding, or, at other times, it can happen as a result of a happy accident or at least occurs as a knock-on effect of acquiring knowledge. But the development of what we need learners to 'be like' to be a successful learner - the dispositions for learning – is often overlooked and rarely discussed. As such, these incredibly important transferrable learning abilities are in danger of passing by unnoticed by both teacher and learner. If this happens, they are also unlikely to be *consciously developed* or *actively transferred* and *applied* in another lesson, situation or domain.

Mastery in learning requires knowledge, understanding, skills *and* the development of the appropriate dispositions that provide a sound foundation upon which to build new knowledge, understanding and skills. An effective learner makes connections between prior, present learning and between the rich variety of learning experiences they encounter as they live their lives because of the dispositions they have developed.

When a disposition is under-developed, then powerful learning opportunities can often be missed.

When we assess the progress of students in well-structured plenary sessions, we have many opportunities to reflect back to them what exactly it is that we can see that tells us how well they are learning and we can check out what they *now* know and understand about what they have learned. In addition, doing so, we can also alert them to the fact that they are now able to *do* something that they were previously unable to do, and possibly suggest times and places when they might find this a useful skill. If we invest time to construct success criteria for a successfully completed task alongside identifying what learners need to 'be like' in order to complete the task, then we can reflect on the learning dispositions alongside the knowledge and understanding in order to show progress when evaluating learning progression.

When we consider the question, 'What is an effective learner?', the responses usually read as a list of dispositions above all else. Here's a list of teacher responses to that question:

Curious, empathetic, kind, reflective, understanding, engaged, optimistic, resilient, aspirational, open-minded, energetic, self aware, enthusiastic, sensitive, thoughtful, imaginative ...

In fact, finding ways to develop these dispositions runs through the very heart of this book. Looking at the list reminds me of what teaching is all about. It goes a long way to capturing the aspiration and hope that we all have for our learners. Maybe it's a list like this that not only attracted us to the job, but keeps us in it?

If learning is going to be the powerful and memorable experience that we all want it to be, and be something that stays with young people far beyond the school gates, we need to design learning opportunities that will explicitly develop learning dispositions. In this way, all learners become consciously aware of what they need to be like in order to acquire new knowledge and develop new skills. In this way, we will be offering them a rich and meaningful menu of opportunities that will develop every aspect of their being as they experience every aspect of school life, whether in their maths, science or music lesson or during their lunch break or going home after school.

Outcome-focused planning

It is through meticulous attention to detail when designing learning that we can focus on the things that really make a difference. If we can make learners consciously aware of 'Where I am now' and 'Where I need to be' then with them we can construct a pathway to 'What I need to do to get there'. Great AfL.[23]

Planning according to our intended outcomes is not about setting learning outcomes in stone, nor is it about prescribing the exact path of travel or mode of transport; it is simply to very deliberately define the direction. This enables us to design learning opportunities that nurture the characteristics of an effective learner. By designing learning in this way, you can calmly and confidently encourage interesting and relevant diversions, whilst always being clear about what you are looking for when it comes to your assessment.

The example overleaf demonstrates how to think through learning design using outcome-focused planning. From the intended outcomes that are anchored on the 'Triple Whammy' planning questions (the 'why' of learning), the design then prompts us to think about how to design learning opportunities to fulfil the stated outcomes (the 'how' of learning). With this framework, there is a prompt to consider explicit ways to involve the learners at the 'share' stage of planning. Finally, the planning question, 'How will I know that (name) has achieved the intended outcome?' requires us to consider how we will recognise and show progress. It can be used to plan individual lessons or for a whole scheme of learning. The point is that the model is a thinking 'frame' upon which we can plan our learning design.

---

23 Black, P. and Wiliam, D., *Inside the Black Box: Raising Standards through Classroom Assessment* (London: King's College, 1988).

Outcome focussed planning tool

Intended outcomes:

1. What does (name) need to know?

The impact of poverty on quality of life in childhood in Brazilian *favelas*

2. What do I want (name) to learn/develop?

CREATIVE THINKING - makes connections/works with others to generate and consider alternative ideas and approaches

3. What does (name) need to be like?

Sensitive: to others' opinions. Flexible: ready to adapt ideas and plans

Opportunities:

What variety of activities/resources can I use?

Use multimedia starter to stimulate discussion

Open-ended 'divergent' thinking tools to generate lots of ideas

Unfamiliar objects are presented to stimulate thinking and discussion

Organise groups according to learning preferences

Recognise achievement:

How will I know that (name) has achieved the intended outcome?

Uses target 'creative thinking' language e.g. 'We considered alternatives' or 'We generated loads of ideas before we settled on this one'.

Makes connections between previously unrelated ideas

Sharing:

How will I share learning intentions/outcomes?

We will construct and agree the success criteria together and agree on these to inform feedback as part of a quality learning conversation

Transferrable learning skills

By asking as an integral planning question, 'What do learners need to *be like?*', we can make explicit reference to the question during the lesson. In this way, the acquisition of learning skills *and* dispositions becomes a very deliberate act. Meanwhile learners are beginning to develop the ability to transfer this across the curriculum and beyond school.

The opportunities provided by integrating learning skills into curriculum design are immense. Here are just a few:

1. Focusing on skills development sharpens our focus on the fundamental question, 'How are we going to organise learning?' We know what we want our pupils to learn *about* (content) but placing an emphasis on 'What do learners need to be able to *do?*' can have a direct impact on the quality of learning design in individual lessons and across the school.

2. By designing learning opportunities in this way, we can also consider how we will *assess* skills development. Using the outcome-focused tool, learning can be designed so that learners have the opportunity to see, practise and develop learning skills. This can lead to far more open-ended learning challenges, higher order thinking and questioning and a lot more learner autonomy.

3. One of the best ways to assess the skills is to talk with students about what they are doing, when they are doing it. As a result, both teachers and students are engaged in more frequent and better quality learning conversations during lessons.

This approach allows us to craft learning with a more 'hands-off' pedagogy, where teachers adopt the role of coach and facilitator and the students get on with the 'doing' of learning.

Integrate assessment at the outset

The following diagram on page 127 is my attempt to visualise the original structure for a long-term project. At the launch of the project, I would explain the brief, set up the groups and pretty much direct the whole process. My aim was to adopt a 'coach-on-the-side' role so from this point on, I would *very gradually* let go. By the end of the second lesson the groups were beginning to set their own targets and work through the scaffolded project brief.

The project certainly produced amazing results from some groups, but often the majority of the class would remain heavily dependent on my interventions and fail to meet even their own deadlines, let alone mine. In addition, I found that I would miss numerous opportunities to celebrate explicitly the skills of collaboration, research and self-management that did occur and, in doing so, I failed to value these skills publicly and certainly didn't assess them either during or at the conclusion of the project. The activity had a linear path, with the occasional diversion created by homework or additional research that a few students would undertake.

One of the primary benefits of deliberately seeking to practise and develop transferrable skills and learning dispositions is that it enables you to integrate whatever you want to assess into the whole project or lesson. This then has a direct impact on the shape or design of learning. With the advent of the PLTS, I was able to redesign the original project structure and map the skills against the project to see what might be celebrated and/or assessed and at what points. Once I had done this, I noticed there were even more opportunities to flag up and highlight specific learning skills and dispositions. I then considered a deliberative approach for the learning skills and began to plan the project in a far more integrated way. The result is illustrated on page 128.

Not only does the project structure change from an inflexible linear model, but also the new format provides discrete opportunities to deliberately focus on the development of those skills and dispositions you want to assess.

Using the 'Triple Whammy' planning approach will lead us to pose questions such as 'What do we need to be like when we are thinking creatively?' or 'What does a good team-worker sound like?' and will enable learners to enhance their

Mapping PLTS against existing work retrospectively

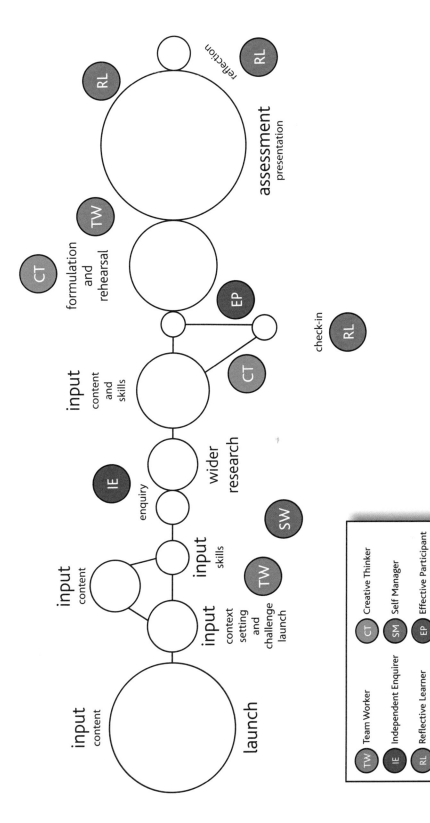

input
content

launch

input
context
setting and
challenge
launch

input
content

input
skills

enquiry

wider
research

input
content
and
skills

check-in

formulation
and
rehearsal

assessment
presentation

reflection

RL

TW

CT

EP

CT

RL

IE

SW

TW

RL

RL

Legend:

TW	Team Worker	CT	Creative Thinker
IE	Independent Enquirer	SM	Self Manager
RL	Reflective Learner	EP	Effective Participant

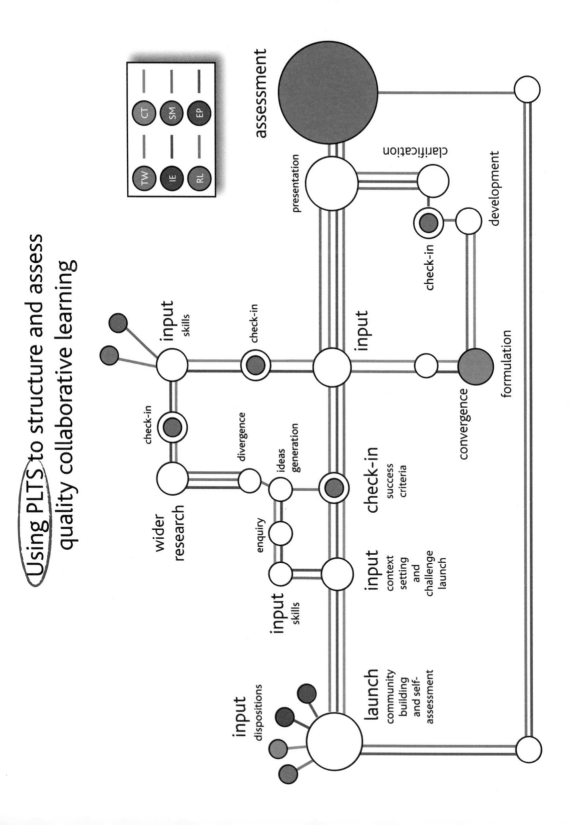

Using PLTS to structure and assess quality collaborative learning

assessment

presentation

clarification

development

check-in

formulation

convergence

input
skills

check-in

input

input
skills

check-in
success
criteria

wider
research

check-in

divergence

ideas
generation

enquiry

input
context
setting
and
challenge
launch

launch
community
building
and self-
assessment

input
dispositions

CT   TW
SM   IE
EP   RL

learning dispositions at the same time as they develop their skills and deepen their knowledge and understanding.

The launch then becomes an opportunity to consider what students need to be able to know, do and be like throughout the project. Traditional 'homework' also then morphs into 'independent enquiry' which, owing to its individual focus, requires deep thinking and can lead to wider research. There are regular opportunities for students to generate ideas, quality assure their progress and deliberately practise their analytical thinking.

The other bonus when designing lessons from the point of view of transferrable learning skills and learning dispositions is the frequent and deliberate opportunities that arise to allow students to practise reflective thinking on both *what* they are learning and *how* they are learning.

Share your learning intentions

It might seem overly pedantic to actively *plan* ways to share our learning intentions, but the unifying principle of Full On Learning is that teaching and learning are two complex and interconnected activities. The successful learner is someone for whom the learning experience has skilfully woven together the dual complexities of teaching *and* learning.

To do this successfully we need to deconstruct teaching skills in order to practise the component parts on our way to teaching mastery. The complexity of learning needs to be dismantled so that we can match the ways we teach to the ways in which children (and adults) learn. This dual deconstruction requires deep reflection, analysis and adaptation. In undertaking this endeavour, we are able to explore what really *does* work and know *why* it works so that we can repeat, innovate and adapt accordingly.

The more we pay conscious, deliberate attention to the approaches we implement, the more likely we are to provide the rationale for why we have chosen that particular approach. At the same time, by paying conscious attention to the 'why' of learning, we can feel reassured and confident that there is a really good reason for it. When we try things out, we often find that we are able to develop alternative approaches and, as we do so, we can ask the learners to trust us. In this way, the learners will understand what we are trying to do, even if the 'how' and the 'what' of what we try doesn't work out.

In Chapter 3, I talked about the relationship between the brain and how we learn – in particular, the importance of being aware of our students' emotional 'age' as we construct learning experiences for them. The brain, which very crudely speaking has a central component with feelings and no language, surrounded by an outer layer of higher functioning capacities including language and the ability to rationalise and make sense of the world, creates what Simon Sinek refers to as the 'three circles model of leadership'.[24] The diagram below shows how we can use this concept of leadership to create a planning tool that identifies distinct opportunities for the deliberate sharing of learning intentions.

Higher order thinking strategies

When it comes to ensuring pace, stretch and challenge, I always take a quick snapshot of what the 'learning landscape' looks like from the perspective of specific learners. Using what I know about the people in front of me - adults and students alike - is the best way to understand what I need to offer in terms of challenge. I then use this picture to shape the learning opportunities I am designing. One example of this 'tweaking' approach to learning design is when I use a framework such as Bloom's Taxonomy as a (sort-of) 'higher order thinking quality assurance system'.[25] I have been able to refresh projects, schemes of learning and programmes of study simply by tweaking. I've given learners their own thinking framework as a prompt for their thinking prior to discussing something like, 'What do we think makes a quality question?' or asking them to be reflexive thinkers ahead of a task; 'What level of thinking is needed when you're completing your chosen task?'. I've also used it in curriculum review work to integrate challenging tasks and compelling

24 Sinek, S., How Great Leaders Inspire Action (September 2009). Available at http://www.ted.com/talks/simon_sinek_how_great_leaders_inspire_action.html.

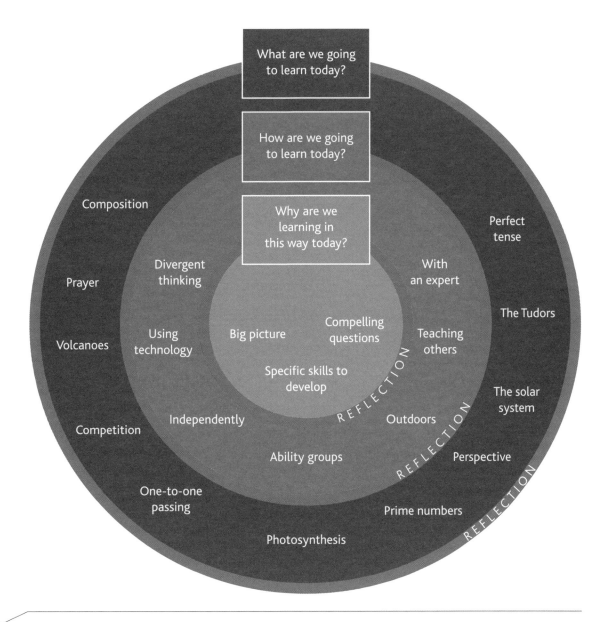

25 More examples ...

Blooms' Taxonomy http://www.learningandteaching.info/learning/bloomtax.htm

Bloom's Revised Taxonomy http://www.kurwongbss.eq.edu.au/thinking/Bloom/blooms.htm

This is great for sharing developing learners' questions. Created by @janeh271 (via Twitter) using Storybird...
http://storybird.com/books/blooming-questions/

Bloom's Digital Taxonomy (Educational Origami) http://edorigami.wikispaces.com/Bloom's+Digital+Taxonomy

INTEL Project: Designing Effective Projects http://www97.intel.com/pk/ProjectDesign/ThinkingSkills/ThinkingFrameworks/

IDEO's Human Centred Design Toolkit http://www.ideo.com/work/human-centered-design-toolkit/

Biggs and Collis http://www.johnbiggs.com.au/solo_taxonomy.html

Creative Thinking Toolkit http://www.coventrypartnership.com/upload/documents/news/PIE%20GROUP/Creative%20Thinking%20
Skills%20-%20Amanda%20Graham.pdf

de Bono's Thinking Hats http://debonoforschools.com/asp/six_hats.asp

Or just Google Bloom's Revised Taxonomy and see what you can find!

questions into schemes of learning. It also works well as an observation tool with very little adaptation. There is a wealth of information available on the web about Bloom's Taxonomy and other thinking frameworks that will support any developmental curriculum design project you might wish to undertake.

When it comes to fostering aspirations, I use a similar quality assurance system. This is my hybrid model of what educational research suggests are the characteristics of a challenging learning environment. As such, I try to ensure that my learning designs can be placed on the right-hand side of the table more often than on the left.

Effective planning and pre-thinking enables teachers to act as facilitators and coaches. It allows the learning process to be made explicit and valued through assessment, reflection and modelling. Effective planning facilitates the development of higher order thinking skills through high order questions – a question-rich environment. This pre-thinking can result in the learning being shaped to individual or group learning needs. This enables the learner to make connections with prior learning, other subjects and transferrable learning skills, attitudes and dispositions.

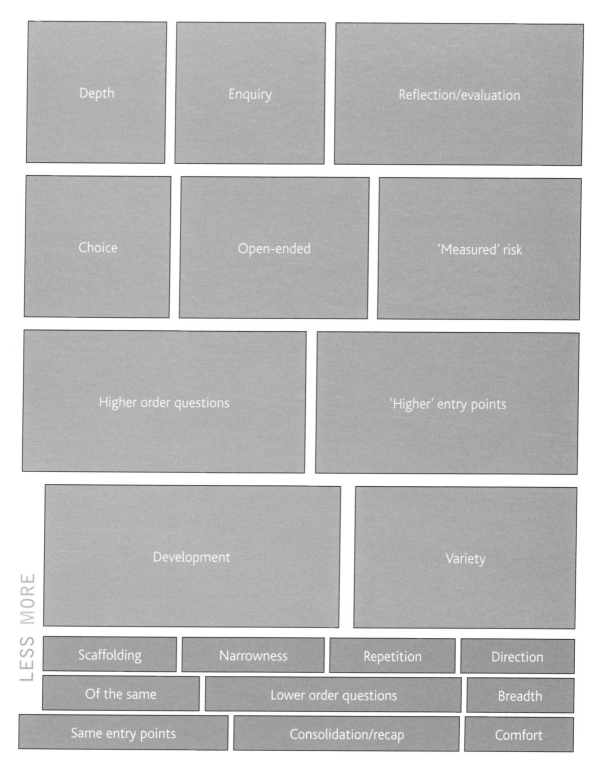

Depth

Enquiry

Reflection/evaluation

Choice

Open-ended

'Measured' risk

Higher order questions

'Higher' entry points

Development

Variety

MORE

LESS

Scaffolding

Narrowness

Repetition

Direction

Of the same

Lower order questions

Breadth

Same entry points

Consolidation/recap

Comfort

FOSTERING ASPIRATION

Design learning through higher order thinking strategies

Explicitly focus on transferrable learning skills

Principles of Full On

Use the 'Triple Whammy' planning question (What do learners need to be able to know and understand? What do they need to be able to do? What do they need to be like?)

Deliberately design specific opportunities for reflection and feedback

Integrate what you want to assess into the task at the outset

Unpack
your own
expertise

Learning Design

Start
at the
end

Deliberately
share your
learning
intentions with
the group

Action Research

How can I develop higher order thinking in *all* learners through my planning strategies?

How do I ensure learning opportunities today make explicit links with other subjects and learning tomorrow and next week?

How do I explicitly value and design opportunities for learners to develop positive learning dispositions alongside cognitive development?

What does an effective learner look like in (subject/topic)?

Focus on

Meticulous thinking: planning strategies/outcome focused/cross-curricular links/ skills and content/planning through questions/learning dispositions

to whatever

comes next

John Cage
(Composer of 4'33" Silent Symphony)

LEARNERS WHO ...	TEACHING THAT ...
Are able to make informed decisions to select and analyse appropriate information and tools to enhance their learning	Provides opportunities for learners to scrutinise the use and application of digital technologies in learning
Openly articulate their thinking processes with others	Encourages the use of appropriate tools (video diaries, podcasting, social media, learning journals, etc.) that focus on the learning *process* rather than the learning *product*
Have the confidence to craft and safeguard a positive digital identity through considered contributions to the digital information space	Offers regular opportunities to focus on developing quality contributions to the creation of new knowledge

LEARNING IN THE DIGITAL AGE

What types of learners do we want to nurture in a digital age?[26]

It is at the point of intersection between the world of exponentially increasing information and where learners access it that is most critical to whether quality learning can take place. The effective leaders and citizens of the 21st century will be those who are able to see connections where previously no link has been made. They will see solutions to the problems which generations have been unable to solve. They will build connections and establish relationships between previously unrelated ideas, people and activities. The characteristics of this dynamic world of information need to be reflected in the behaviours of our learners today – ready for tomorrow. Just as the World Wide Web is flexible, creative and surprising, so the capacities of those who are set to make best use of it need to be flexible, creative and surprisingly adept at problem-solving. This chapter focuses on the learning dispositions and skills that young people need to develop in a digital-rich world. In many ways, these skills and dispositions are not distinctively 'digital', rather their importance has become greater as a result of the incredible growth of the digital world.

---

26 Inspired by a talk by Michael Wesch at TEDxNYED, New York, 6 March 2010 (webcast)

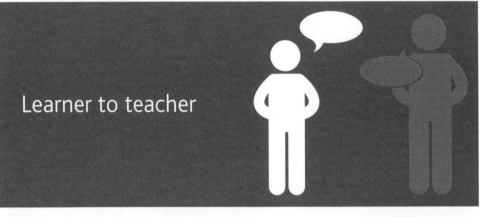

Mashing up knowledge (the new-from-old learning model)

The digital world is characterised by flux. It is dynamic in its ability to rapidly construct new knowledge in a collaborative, open and creative way. This is just what our classrooms need to be like. They should be safe spaces where quality feedback allows for discoveries to be transformed collaboratively into new understandings. Learners can then engage with new questions, challenges and concepts, applying their newly developed skills to fresh learning tasks. It is just these learning capacities that are transferrable into the digital world, and back again.

The 21st century digital learner

More than an insatiable thirst for knowledge-consumption, the effective learner has a desire to construct *new* knowledge. And then *share* this knowledge with the wider world. They have the necessary insight to see and then create connections between pre-existing knowledge in apparently unrelated spheres and from it make something new. They want to not only consume knowledge *but also* own it, play with it, adapt it and reconstitute it - mash it up - for their own unique purposes. This might be in the form of a sampled piece of music transformed into a new composition, a LOL Cats contribution[27] or a video mash-up of Tony Blair and George W. Bush played over 'Endless Love' to create a highly entertaining satirical political commentary.[28] Effective learners are creators *and* consumers in this sophisticated world. And so are effective educators.

All of this reflects a shift that has taken place thanks to Web 2.0 technologies. Whereas a relatively short time ago my dad struggled to create his own email account, he now regularly uses Facebook to keep in touch with the rest of the family, his smartphone to upload photos of his latest golf successes and regularly texts

27 See http://icancheezburger.com
28 See http://www.youtube.com/watch?v=UtEH6wZXPA4.

me bad jokes that only my dad could find funny. He, like most of us, was a fairly passive consumer of information barely five years ago. Now, Web 2.0 has enticed him, as it has with many of us, to become active participants and creators of our own content. We have graduated from being down-loaders to up-loaders.

The 'mash-up' culture provides fertile ground for creative, imaginative and 'different thinking' individuals and groups to explore and collaborate. To get the most from it, the ability to make creative (and safe) connections has never been more important along with, like you find with any good children's birthday party, an idea of what you have to 'take home' at the end of the day. What is it that is new and unique that has been created as a result of this learning experience? This leads to the simplest of all plenary questions 'What are you leaving with today that you didn't have before you came in?' If you've done your job properly, you'll find the answer is often, 'A headache' but, in the main, you'll start to get some thoughtful and self-aware responses. As a result, you can be assured that your teaching has had an impact on learning and that progression has occurred.

Using technology effectively to enhance learning is all about finding the right digital tools that will enrich and enhance – but not dominate - the learning. As a result, learning productivity can soar. It is fair to say that 'Under-18' does not necessarily equate to 'digitally literate', but there is certainly a willingness and confidence in our learners to use new digital tools. Whether this is a low-tech video camera, a mobile phone or a digital camera, we and our learners now, more than ever, have the opportunity and confidence to capture personal learning moments and share them with an audience-size that is beyond imagination of most of us even five years ago.

Games-informed learning

In designing learning opportunities, you will always be trying to hook into the intrinsic motivation of your learners. It seems to make sense then, that we should take a look at what some of our students currently do, by their own volition, and steal what we can from the world of games and play. In doing so, we can have a go at tapping into the characteristics of engagement that keep young people immersed, enthralled and fully concentrated for hours on end.

All good games, whether they are parlour, board or computer games, reflect much of what we know about how we learn. The joy of playing games rests in the opportunity to compete and interact, expressing individual capacities within a mutually-agreed structure – a mess-within-a-box approach. In game-playing, we know that participants feel both appropriately challenged and sufficiently safe to experiment and develop strategies to get through any 'stuck' stages. As such, they'll stick with it.

Take a glance at some of the most popular digital games on platforms such as the Wii, PSP, Nintendo or Playstation and we can unravel what it is that makes them so successful. After all, these are activities that people voluntarily give up hours of their precious time to play. By borrowing what we know about human behaviour from the world of games design and incorporating it into the way we design learning, we can start to craft connections between the why, the how and the what of learning. So, imagine designing a scheme of learning that seeks to explicitly promote the following component parts.

The list in the following table is a hybrid of personal insights from a number of fantastic educators, creative designers and educational researchers with whom I have had the pleasure of working during my career, but it is by no means exhaustive.

Time for reflection

Opportunities to take a step back, recognise progress and redraft success criteria for any task so as to develop a sense of incremental achievement.

Example: Learning blogs. Provide learners with a space in which they can write their personal reflections and receive feedback from their peers, parents, carers and the global community. You can provide prompt questions to develop their ability to reflect on the process of their learning and the development of their dispositions, alongside their cognitive development. There are also excellent AfL opportunities through self- and peer-assessment.

Transfer (skills and knowledge)

Ability to experience new contexts and domains where newly acquired skills can be adapted and applied. This supports emotional safety as even though the task is new, the skills required to meet the challenge are familiar.

Example: Rehearse-review-apply. By creating scenarios using a 'mantle of the expert', hot seat or problem simulation activity you will provide learners with an opportunity to rehearse questioning, thinking and behaving 'as'. Contextual learning opportunities where the learning has real implications help to encourage an understanding of relevance. For example, if the school is receiving a delivery, organisational, interpersonal and a range of other skills and aptitudes can be practised if learners are invited to take the lead in certain aspects of everyday life of the school.

Mystery

Although aspects of the task should be open and clear, there are also some elements of surprise and revelation along the way to maintain interest and prevent repetition.

Example: Treasure hunt tactics. Provide three key pieces of information required to complete or answer a task. Disguise or hide the remaining key pieces of information around the school, in text/ pictures (QR or quick response codes are great for this) or provide various groups with different pieces of information. The only way to solve the challenge is to negotiate, persuade or influence other groups to reveal what they know in exchange for what you know. Alternatively, you could time the release of key pieces of information, requiring students to be in a particular place at a particular time to discover the facts they need.

Problem-solving

Fostering innate curiosity through question posing and intrigue feeds higher order thinking such as analysis, speculation, the application of new skills and creation of new knowledge.

Example: What if? question generator. Using the simple 'What if?' strategy, ask learners to generate three questions in response to a topic or subject-related stimulus (e.g. picture, object, sound, film clip). As a whole group they have to construct the most challenging (higher order) questions and then research and present answers to each other's questions within a given time frame and formulate an enquiry around the most challenging questions.

Rapid response

Providing time limits helps with clearly defined rules and success criteria. In addition, time limits can promote a sense of urgency and the satisfaction of knowing that each task is finite.

Example: Gantt Chart learning. Ask learners to map the time available to them against the tasks they have to complete. A large-scale Gantt Chart on a piece of graffiti-paper works well as a whole-class visual and allows each learner/group to monitor their progress against others. Ensure learners are involved in the creation of milestones for their learning as these will offer discrete opportunities for on-going reflection and quality feedback during the task.

Challenge

Challenge should be offered in a variety of ways. There may be challenge either in having to collaborate to accomplish a task or in completing it individually (emotional and dispositions). There may be challenge in the task itself and the skills required to complete it (cognitive and intellectual) or the time limits given.

Example: Challenge target. Ask learners to check-in on the target where they think they are during the task and be specific about the way in which they feel challenged (if they do).

Structured scaffolding

Incremental skill acquisition allows participants to meet the requirements of every task at gradually increasing levels. Only when they have attained the necessary skills and experience in one task are they able to move on to the next. This is decided upon by the integrated nature of the assessment criteria.

Example: Bloom's Taxonomy/PLTS/thinking framework as a planning tool. Share a clear picture of what progression looks like with associated success criteria. Use the planning tool as a framework to underpin the level of challenge and make this explicit in each task.

Social aspect/ community

Participants engage with the task together, as part of a community. They experience the same successes and struggles in a safe and highly engaged environment.

Example: Redesign your groups. Allow the learning outcome to inform the group design. Ask groups to assign each other roles and ensure they agree success criteria before they embark on the task.

Feedback

Quality feedback characterises the participant's journey. The feedback is focused, deliberate and mindful of the completion of the task.

Example: Observing learning. In the role of observer, the teacher (or learner) can stand back and offer regular quality feedback informed by what they see and hear. This can be unobtrusive if you use sticky notes and a class feedback wall or graffiti wall. Alternatively, www.wallwisher.com is an online tool that's useful to collate feedback. Add to this links, further ideas and photos to create a collage of learning for the whole group.

Goals

Short, medium and longer term targets are made clear to the participant throughout their journey. This means there is always an opportunity to achieve, develop and acquire recognition in skill acquisition.

Example: Storyboard my learning. Imagine the lesson is a storyboard for an episode of *CSI*. Use reflective questioning to encourage forward planning, 'What do you hope to achieve/find out/be able to do ... in 10 minutes and how will you know you've done this?' Have regular check-ins to identify working-towards targets for individual learners (this could be sticky notes on a target or a learning wall) and link all of these into the final plenary. The narrative for the lesson at this point will be completed with 'To be continued ...' as the next steps. Radar charts are another way to pinpoint specific goals and are referred to as a progress-checker.

Adaptability/ individualisation	Every participant's journey is created by them, leaving their own 'learning footprint' on their progress route.
	Example: What's the problem? Encourage learners to design their own tasks and formulate their own problems. Ask them to set realistic deadlines linked to success criteria. The online platform/ tool www.voicethread.com enables a continuous discussion to be recorded, with links posted and responses offered. It is an excellent way to promote quality learning conversations and reinforce the idea that learning is continuous (it is also great for CPD). A similar tool is www.primarypad.com, which works well to support collaborative work and meetings.
Progress	Explicit milestones shared with the participants develop a sense of achievement and goals throughout the task.
	Example: Learning timeline. Pinpoint exactly what *you* expect to be achieved and when. Make sure this is displayed and accessible to all learners so they can get on with their learning rather than having to keep asking you or you having to constantly remind them. Link this to the wider context of learning so the why is just as clear as the how and the what.

So ... how do we make learning look, sound and feel like this, so that it enhances deeper knowledge acquisition and understanding and develops specific learning skills and behaviours in all our learners?

The table contains indicators that are not that dissimilar from what we might consider to be characteristic of *any* compelling learning opportunity. If we translate these into practical strategies you use when we design learning, we may also find that we tap into the emotional learning strategies of our learners by giving them the why, how and what of the lesson.

A different kind of learner?

As with every generation, the world in which learners are becoming adults is not the same as the world in which we grew up. The digital world brings with it infinite opportunities to collaborate, innovate and reinvent; to think through play. Information no longer has a gatekeeper. So we have a new role in the classroom, and with this role comes a new skill-set. With all this democratisation, we need to be skilful enough to quality-assure the information in order to help learners make informed decisions and insightful selections about what they take notice of and what they dismiss. We must be guardians of the *creation* of knowledge. We must require learners to apply rigorous selection criteria to what they choose to share and upload as well as when and how they interact with others and how they create and maintain their own online presence. The tricky thing is that this is very different from how most teachers experienced learning themselves or, indeed, what we were originally trained to believe our role was all about.

Observing the many ways in which young people interact with new technologies on a daily basis gives us further evidence of how they respond productively to those things in which they find personal satisfaction, space for self-expression and opportunities for engagement. Just think about the skills of a 14-year-old as they multitask with their personal technology – forging connections, co-creating content and making new links as they shape their corner of the digital world. They have complete design freedom over this space. They can exercise control over who they invite in, what they select to populate their space with and how they express themselves within it.

This is just one of the ways in which childhood has dramatically changed as a result of the digital world. As a result, we need to find ways to respond to the undeniable fact that the more freedom we taste, the more we want. This is particularly true if the freedom we experience is well managed and structured so that it is the most productive and safe that we can make it. Children have more freedom and self-expression far earlier in their lives than ever before too. This freedom inevitably brings with it challenges and responsibilities for us as adults to safeguard their emotional safety and well-being. Whilst their technological ability far exceeds that of their peers a decade ago, their life experience, in the main, does not.

In fact, it could be argued that the downside of their technological advancement is that time spent in a digital world has prevented 'real' life experiences (such as outdoor play, game-making and other risk-taking activities) and thereby hampered the development of protective strategies. Digital literacy does not equate with emotional literacy. That aside, it is second nature to learners today to use their technological skills and confidence to shape their world and dictate their free time.

Enabling students to become 'knowledge-able'

As we increasingly move toward an environment of instant and infinite information, it becomes less important for students to know, memorize, or recall information, and more important for them to be able to find, sort, analyze, share, discuss, critique, and create information. They need to move from being simply knowledgeable to being knowledge-able.

Michael Wesch[29]

29 Wesch, M., From Knowledgeable to Knowledge-able: Experiments in New Media Literacy. Keynote speech, ELI Annual Conference, Orlando, Florida, 21 January 2009. Available at http://www.academiccommons.org/commons/essay/knowledgable-knowledge-able.

Michael Wesch is Assistant Professor of Cultural Anthropology at Kansas State University. In spring 2007 he asked his students to share their responses to the question, 'What do you think of your education?' The outcome was a film about '21st century learners' that subsequently went viral on the internet and became a staple for all school and conference INSETs.[30] Using his expertise in anthropological enquiry, Wesch used the exercise as the basis for analysing the ways in which information acquisition is markedly different for young people in education today in comparison with even ten years ago. In his subsequent writings and talks, he uses the quotation above as a call to action, emphasising the need for teachers to enable learners to become 'knowledge-able'.

If we are to inspire learning within the world as it really is, then our pedagogy and curriculum must adapt to enable the smooth integration of technology to *enhance* learning. A flexible curriculum should lead to the subtle and slow-burn adoption of technology that is fairly unobtrusive. In this way, digital language and tools can be fully integrated into the learning experiences we design.

It is testimony to the extraordinary power of human creativity that any attempt to compile a list of tools and applications currently available would be like sailing against a relentless headwind. This is the world that we are all already in.

> Today applications cover all aspects of life, helping users do everything from managing budgets, locating the perfect restaurant, viewing the latest weather forecasts, and updating their social media accounts. Recent statistics say there are 263,088 apps currently available for download, with games market being the most lucrative.

> Adam Burns[31]

A brilliant example of this subtle integration of the digital world is the rapidly growing availability of Web 2.0 applications, open-source tools and mobile technologies. The best of these tools can be adapted in a no-tech way because at their heart is just a really good idea. Wallwisher (www.wallwisher.com) is a digital version of

---

30 *A Vision of Students Today* is available at http://www.youtube.com/watch?v=dGCJ46vyR9o.
31 Adam Burns *A Bite of the Apple,* http://www.meettheboss.tv/Article/46/A-Bite-of-the-Apple/ Posted 22 September 2010

a 'sharing wall' that can be used as a simple feedback wall or Twitter feed (www. twitter.com) in any lesson with the added advantage of being able to display videos, images and audio files. The wall can be added to by anybody from anywhere in the world at any time of day or night. It can be saved and kept as a document of learning for future reference. It is a powerful option for blurring the boundaries between the classroom and the world beyond.

The inventors of some of the most influential tools have often been unable to imagine the far-reaching potential of their creations until they are placed into the hands of users. This is the way in which the telephone and the internet came into being and how Web 2.0 technology has evolved. The principle is that *any* good learning idea can be adapted to enhance *any* kind of learning. And if we ask our learners to think of ways to adapt and expand on these ideas – to truly involve them – then who knows what fantastic developments will be born.

What to do and what to be like

The digital skill-set that learners now require is not characterised by knowledge *acquisition* but knowledge *creation*. It is predicated on the assertion that 'the knowledge' probably already exists, so there is no need for one person to act as gatekeeper and granting access to the fortunate few. Knowledge is well on its way to being democratised, if it isn't there already.[32] The secret is to find it, sort it, select it and use it to create and express our own understanding of the world. To be fair, there is little difference between this and the approach to knowledge endorsed by Socrates. If, as Socrates asserted, 'The wisest man is he who knows he knows nothing', then those of us referred to as 'digital immigrants' can rest assured that we are probably pretty wise when it comes to digital literacy.

---

32 Dweck, C. S., *Mindset: The New Psychology of Success* (New York: Random House, 2006).

The trick to pull off in our teaching and lesson design is how to:

 Make best use of this resource by directly involving those in the know (the learners) and being courageous enough to do this.

 Nurture and develop the necessary digital skills and competencies that are needed by our learners to both confidently *and* safely navigate the digital world. We need to do this for ourselves *first* so we're confident enough to involve our learners in the same process.

 Ensure that *any* lack of confidence on our part serves *only to encourage* us to keep learning.

Digital discernment

Before opening up a browser window, we need to think about what we're looking for, how we will know when we've found it and reflect on the quality of whatever it is we discover. The ability to discern has never been in greater demand. With ever more information coming our way, how do we judge the quality (authenticity, credibility, accuracy, relevance, etc.) of the information we have before us? And how do we help our learners do the same?

If I think back to my first explorations of the internet, I remember wasting hours trawling through page after page of search results. I would often visit every site only to discover that, although it wasn't directly relevant, it was very interesting and perhaps I should keep reading, just in case there was something crucial to discover. Nowadays, I can't remember the last time I looked beyond the first page of a Google search – I barely skim-read the first few entries and very rarely go beyond that.

So what has changed? Familiarity, yes. But above all, I have become far more selective about the information I choose to use. I am also reassured (rightly or wrongly) that search engines have got better. They are faster and more intuitive and dynamic in how they work. Nowadays, even as you type your enquiry, you are given some pointers to improve the accuracy of your search.

Through experience and learning, I have developed my own criteria for what I consider to be 'good' or 'quality' information. Although most of the learners we work with appear 'naturally' to be at ease with internet searches and have very high levels of confidence and familiarity with this world, I have one distinct advantage over them. I had to *deliberately learn* to navigate the digital landscape with no prior experience. As a result I have retained a small but important droplet of suspicion about the online world – a hint of discernment that many of our learners need to acquire. We need to check-in with learners to ensure that they actively question the authenticity of what they find.

Discerning questions

Learners need to regularly ask questions of the type that will be familiar to anybody who has taught about analysing the reliability of sources. Here are some examples (by no means an exhaustive list) of discerning questions that we need to encourage learners to ask when they are using information from the web.[33]

What exactly do I want/need to find out?

Do I want facts, opinions, reported accounts, interpretations, statistics, etc.?

How reliable is this source? Have I got good reasons to trust this source?

Is this information objective, subjective or unclear?

Who is the author of this information?

---

33 This list a hybrid of several evaluation-checkers you can find on the internet, like this one http://eduscapes.com/tap/topic32.htm.

dis·cern·ment/

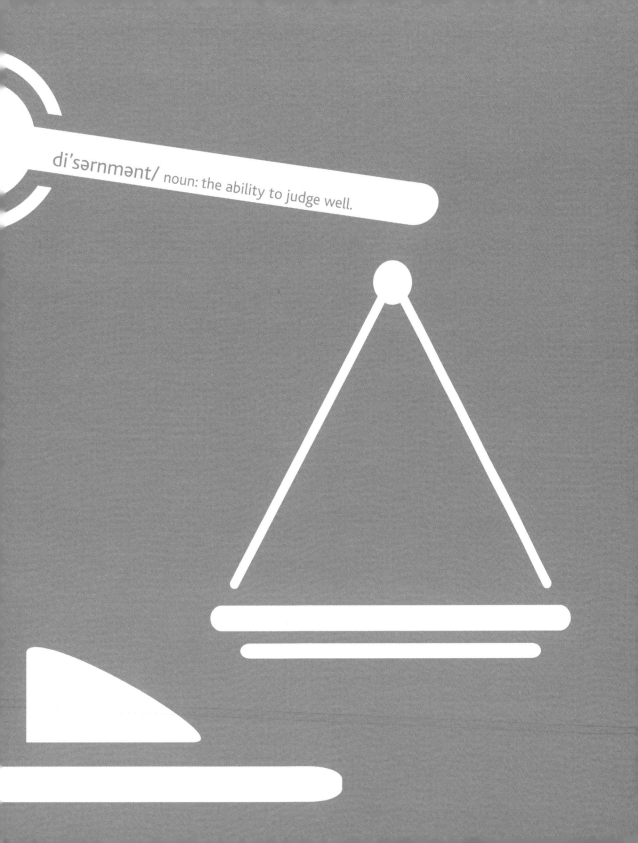

di'sərnmənt/ noun: the ability to judge well.

When was this information posted/updated?

Is there a sponsor of this page/website – what do I know about them?

Why is this information here and what is its purpose?

Is this information first-hand or second-hand?

What do I need to consider before I use this source in *my* work?

Can I check out the contact or bibliographical information or find out more about the organisation/author of this information?

What criteria do I need to test the quality, credibility and reliability of this information?

Does this information provide me with new knowledge or reinforce existing knowledge?

Is there prejudice, bias or a hidden agenda in this information?

Are there similar pages or sources that support what I've found here?

Process–generation–application

To develop the skill of discernment, learners must be given deliberate opportunities to practise the *process* of posing questions, then *generate* ideas and tentative solutions in response to these and then being able to *apply* discernment in the way, the process of information selection. There are opportunities for discernment-development to be found in pretty much every curriculum area. Just as much as it always has been for generations past, the need to question ourselves, check our understanding and provide evidence for our conclusions is an integral part of learning. Perhaps even more so in the digital and ideas age.

The principles of games-design to enhance learning

WHAT HAPPENS IN GAMES	WHAT IT LOOKS LIKE IN LEARNING DESIGN
Personal fulfilment **Intrinsic motivation** **Autonomy**	**Learners make decisions about their own learning** **Learners are encouraged to construct their own problems to solve**
In really successful games, players choose their own routes and make their own decisions. There are high levels of intrinsic motivation where the player is encouraged to keep playing as a result of a sense of *personal fulfilment* once they have made their own decisions about how to proceed. The successes (and failures) begin to really matter. The reward of playing the game is that the player gets better at the game, so there is a strong sense of self-satisfaction to feed continued engagement in the game.	Every learner makes some decisions about the way in which they learn. (There's more about this in Chapter 10 on Motivation). Suffice to say, it's the Four Ts: Choices may be limited to one or two of *time*: the time they have to complete the task; *activity*: the way in which they will learn; *outcome*: the type of 'product' they present at the end; *group*: the people with whom they can work. The learning journey is created *by* and *with* them that leaves a personal 'learning footprint' on their progress route. Learners are asked to design elements of their own tasks and formulate their own problems by using the minimum amount of information.[34] Additional information is gradually revealed as and when they really need it. For example, ask them to identify 'What's the problem?' in an appropriate word or a picture as a start point. Alternatively, pose a series of information-revealing questions to encourage them to (a) construct their own problems and (b) solve them for/with each other: 1 What do we already know that will help us with this? 2 What do we need to know that we *don't* know? 3 What information that we now have really matters to us if we are to solve this? 4 So what *is* the problem?

34 This is inspired by Dan Meyer www.mrmeyer.com and TEDxNYED www.ted.com/talks/dan_meyer_math_curriculum_makeover.html 'Math class needs a makeover' Posted May 2010.

| | Increase the expected levels of responsibility by requiring them to identify the success criteria, 'What would a quality outcome look like?' and set realistic deadlines linked to success criteria. This works well in promoting quality learning conversations *and* reinforcing the idea that learning is the learners' job and as such, every component part of it is continuous. |

Progress is publicly recognised

Teachers and learners question each other to develop and articulate thinking 'out loud'

Learning journals and/blogs are used to support reflection and seek feedback during lessons

WHAT HAPPENS IN GAMES	WHAT IT LOOKS LIKE IN LEARNING DESIGN
All games rely on players experiencing a strong sense of accomplishment and achievement that is publicly acknowledged within a group of fellow game-players and possibly an audience of spectators.	There are frequent opportunities for teachers and learners to take a step back, recognise progress and redraft success criteria for any task so as to develop a sense of *incremental* achievement.
	Provide learners with time and space to write personal learning reflections. If it's a safely set up and well-managed blog, the scope of feedback they can receive will extend beyond their peers, parents, carers to the global community.
	Provide prompt questions to support the development of their reflective capacities and the development of their dispositions.
	This will also enhance their cognitive development.
	Shared journals are also excellent AfL opportunities through self- and peer-assessment.
	The online platform/tool www.voicethread.com enables a continuous discussion to be recorded, with links posted and responses offered.

Transfer of skills and knowledge to new situations
Acquisition of new information/objects/tools

Great games offer players an ability to experience new contexts and domains where they can apply their newly acquired skills. This means that even though the task is new, the skills required to meet the challenge are familiar and practised.

New skills and knowledge may be virtual or actual to help the player with a range of game-specific challenges, but there is also inherent cognitive and physical skill development as the game continues.

Explicit opportunities are designed for learners to (a) refine (b) apply what they have learnt to new situations
Learners recognise the new skills they have acquired

Learners asked to check out their understanding with each other in new situations.

Learners are encouraged to reflect on and identify 'What I can now do/know/understand that I couldn't/didn't at the start of the lesson.'

By creating scenarios using a 'mantle of the expert', 'hot seat', role plays, decision-making exercises or real-life simulation activities, learners can rehearse questioning, refine their knowledge, understanding and skills, deepen their thinking and behave 'as'.

Contextual learning opportunities encourage learners to recognise that their learning has real implications so that they see its relevance.

Incremental levels of challenge
Structured scaffolding

During game-play, levels are built into the game so it gradually gets harder. The structure of these levels is clear to the player, so they know where they are, where they want to be and are able to un-pick what it is that they need to do to achieve their goal. Short, medium and long-term targets are made clear to the participant throughout their journey.

This means there is always an opportunity to achieve, develop and acquire recognition in skill acquisition. The player is unable to move onto the next level until they are ready and have completed the previous level. This means that challenge comes at a pace that suits the player.

Assessment criteria are explicit at the start of the task. Learners know how well they are doing and what they need to do to improve

Learners welcome the variety of challenges they experience during the lesson

Regular progress checks ensure that challenge is appropriately pitched for all learners

Learners experience challenge in a variety of ways, for example:

Emotional and dispositional: learners may have to *collaborate* to accomplish a task within a group OR have to complete it *individually*.

Cognitive and intellectual: the content of the task itself, or the skills needed to complete it or the time limits given.

Using a 'challenge target' of some sort helps as a regular progress-checker. Learners have to identify how challenged they feel during the lesson by using the target (Centre: comfort zone; Outer ring: Danger Zone; Middle ring: Challenge Zone) see page 199.

Storyboarding learning is a useful way to capture and reflect on the goals that learners have achieved. Imagine the lesson is a storyboard for an episode of *CSI*. You can restrict this to as many boxes as you like, from one 'Headline' box that captures a key learning moment to a series of three to six completed over a period of time. The 'next steps' for the lesson at this point can be framed as a 'To be continued' or 'Next lesson: the Revenge ...'.

Reflective questioning can be used to encourage forward planning, 'What do you hope to achieve/find out/be able to do ... in the next 5/10/15 minutes? How will you know you've been successful?' Using regular check-ins will identify working-towards targets for individual learners (this could be sticky notes on a target or a learning wall) and link into a final plenary.

Problem-solving
Sense of achievement

Learners feel confident to try out a range of possible solutions and are encouraged to assess the implications of one solution over another

Lessons require a high level of 'question-posing' and testing of ideas and solutions before the 'best' solution is agreed upon

Lessons establish a question-rich environment through teachers and learners persistently posing questions.

Learners can use the following process to shape their thinking:

- Present problem

- Generate a range of possible solutions (divergent thinking)

- Identify a solution to test (convergent thinking)

- Test solution against success criteria

- Analyse responses (feedback)

- Construct or refine a new problem

Frameworks are used that encourage higher order thinking and encourage learners to 'question-the-question' in order to pose their responses to the problem.

Learners are confident enough to try, test and explore alternative solutions in the process of problem-solving.

Some of the most successful games present the player with a series of decision-making exercises. They have to assess the possible implications of their choices in order to make decisions about the path they will choose. They work things out by trying, failing and trying again. Often, they are presented with obscure problems that demand high degrees of lateral thinking in order to find a solution and move on. They remain engaged because their actions are underpinned by a sense that they WILL achieve the goals they have set themselves.

WHAT HAPPENS IN GAMES	WHAT IT LOOKS LIKE IN LEARNING DESIGN
	Learners are able to speculate next steps, suggest possible outcomes and assess implications ('If that happens, then this will happen...').

They can use this information to create new scenarios to test-out.

Using a simple 'What if?' strategy, learners can identify three possible problems in response to a topic or subject-related stimulus (e.g. picture, object, sound, film clip). They can think and discuss together to construct the 'best' solutions measured against success criteria and then present their response to the problem posed. |
| **Mystery and immersion**
Active Learning
Social Learning

At the heart of 'play' and any games, in fact, whether they are traditional board games, sport or digital games, is the opportunity for the players to become immersed in the challenge at hand.

The 'hook' for many games is the inclusion of unexpected revelations or incomplete information that will only become whole when levels are completed or skills are acquired. | **Learners are excited by the learning process and actively seek out and share their understanding with each other**
Learners take responsibility for constructing their own knowledge and collaborate with each other to achieve an agreed and shared goal

Although aspects of the task should be open and clear, there are also some elements of surprise and revelation along the way to maintain interest and prevent repetition.

Learning outcomes inform the group design. Where new skills are the focus for the lesson, learners of similar abilities are encouraged to learn together. Where the focus for the lesson is problem-solving, diverse ability groupings are used to ensure different ways of thinking are included.

When groups are constructed, roles are assigned to ensure key responsibilities are distributed within the group.

Learners agree success criteria, time limits, resources needed etc. before they embark on the task. |

Using 'Treasure Hunt Tactics' is a helpful way to encourage learners to complete the bigger picture for themselves:

- Provide three key pieces of information required to complete or answer a task.

- Disguise or hide the remaining key pieces of information around the classroom/school/in text/on websites/in pictures (QR or quick response codes are great for this).

- Provide groups with different pieces of information.

- The only way to solve the challenge is to use the skills of negotiation to persuade other groups to reveal what they know in exchange for what your group knows.

- Alternatively, you could stagger the release of key pieces of information during the lesson, requiring students to be in a particular place at a particular time to discover the facts they need.

In any game, there is a delicate balance of competition and collaboration. Players engage with the task together, as part of a community. They have a sense of belonging as a result of sharing a goal. They adhere to the same rules and they experience the same successes and struggles in a safe and highly engaged environment.

Action Research

How do I deliberately use technology to encourage learners to see and make new connections, to analyse, to reflect and to draw conclusions that they hold up to scrutiny, test, check and reform?

How can I guide learners to make appropriate, safe and well-informed decisions about their future?

What would a 14-year-old choose to have in their curriculum that would be relevant to them – for now and for the future I can imagine?

What subjects and skills would they want to learn to ensure they are prepared for a new world?

How can I incorporate the 'exciting stuff' (digital games, social media, new technologies, etc.) to enhance the ways in which students learn?

How could I resource a play-enabled curriculum? What pedagogy would I need to develop in order to accommodate it? What would individual lessons start to look like?

How would I measure progress in 'playful thinking' and ensure it supported knowledge-acquisition?

How would I ensure that 'expert' input resulted in 'expert' output? And who would the 'experts' be?

What do learners voluntarily spend their free time doing? How can I design learning that connects with this? (This is where they are most likely going to get their 10,000 hours to develop expertise in digital confidence and competence.)

How can I find out and use what exactly it is about social networking that keeps young people engaged?

In what ways can I learn from the engagement principles behind Facebook and apply these to learning design (developing networks, working collaboratively (e.g. Farmville), expressing personality, likes and dislikes, sharing photos, key events, important moments, etc.)?

 In what ways could I create a 'research schedule' instead of a syllabus (constructing essential questions, lines of enquiry, quality learning conversations, etc.)? How would I assess progress using such an approach and how would it serve existing curriculum goals?

How could I encourage research to be undertaken collaboratively by the whole school community (defining our roles, practising and reflecting on *how* learning takes place and the learning relationships I create through these experiences)?

How could I crowd-source learning using the principle that 30 learners will glean and inform us of at least 30 times the amount of understanding that one teacher can (gather their views, their perspectives, their interpretations and their opinions to inform the quality of our provision)?

Language

... begins with listening

Jeanette Winterson

LEARNERS WHO ...	TEACHING THAT ...
Deliberately practise their own expertise within and beyond school	Offers a varied diet that develops specific skills in different contexts, with different team members at different times

Focus: Quality feedback cycle |
| Believe that they get better through hard work, not luck. Set their own targets and believe they can always improve | Praises effort within a task, rather than the individual attainment of the learner, 'Clever is what clever does'

Focus: Learning language |
| Use focused feedback from teachers and peers to develop their own expertise | Encourages quality learning conversations, developing a reflective-centric classroom focused on learning

Focus: Feedback |

FEEDBACK

Seek, collate and respond

The importance of feedback in the learning process sits proudly near pole position of every single 'What makes the difference?' race-grid of teaching and learning interventions.[35] To ignore feedback is to overlook the most integral part of the learning process and miss out on the opportunity to draw out the capacity to enquire in every learner. We can pour all our energy into designing fantastic, compelling learning opportunities, we can stand back, let the learning happen and be delighted at the achievements of our learners, but unless we take deliberate steps to actively seek out how well the learning is 'sticking' in the minds of our learners, we will never really know how effective our strategies are. By seeking information about learners' thinking we can increase our 'learning intelligence'. The questions we invite our learners to ask of *themselves*, of *each other* and of *us* teaches learners how to construct knowledge and forge exciting new connections for themselves. It values curiosity as an integral component of the learning process.

This enables us to lead valuable continuous assessments so that we know exactly what steps to take to ensure we draw out the most powerful learning capacities of our learners. And to repeat them.

---

35 See John Hattie's book *Visible Learning* (Abingdon: Routledge, 2009) and his website at http://www.education. auckland.ac.nz/uoa/home/about/staff/j.hattie.

Dual feedback channels

An effective learner will *demand* focused feedback from their teachers and their peers. It is up to us to build in regular opportunities for them to rehearse this. As learners explore new ideas, we can encourage them to engage in speculation and hypothetical thinking to deepen their understanding. We need to hear this thinking (either through verbal or written dialogue) to nurture and feed their innate curiosity. It is the learning opportunities *learners themselves* go on to create and the questions *they* pose that will make progress possible and visible to us (and them). Our teaching skill relies on our ability to draw out what is already in the hearts and minds of our learners. If we listen and ask, we are best placed to help them shape their unformed ideas and involve them in their own sense-making journey. If they are going to reveal their learning capacities and passions on this journey, they need to be able to respond to and create their own powerful questions. Quality feedback provides these opportunities.

Feedback channel 1: Learner to learner

It is always fascinating to watch young people assess themselves and one another, offer advice and teach each other what they need to do in order to master their goals. I live around the corner from a very popular skate-park where I have seen this kind of learner-led interaction and communication in action. Admittedly, much of it is barely audible and when you can make out more than a grunt it rarely expands beyond a 10 to 15 second exposition. I recently overhead a young skateboarder saying to his parents on the way home, 'I learnt, like, *eight* tricks today … oh my God, it was awesome.' To which one of his parents responded, 'That's really excellent, I'm really proud of you.' Having seen the skaters in action, I know that he will have learnt those tricks from trying out moves, taking risks, building his confidence, seeking and receiving feedback and being determined to get it right. All of which will have taken place within a group of fellow skateboarders, of varying ages, backgrounds and abilities. A high level blend of independent and collaborative learning is underpinned by the quality of feedback and learning dialogue within the group. I often wonder what learning would look, feel and sound like if it constantly offered learning opportunities that enabled the same sort of exploratory learning conversations and feedback that take place on an average Saturday afternoon at my local skate-park.

The most exciting learning emerges when learners are able to discuss their thinking together. Through the articulation of their thinking, students can check their understanding against that of their peers. This is when they truly involve themselves in taking control of – that is to say ownership of and responsibility for - their learning and begin to drive it for themselves. It is at this point that we can be reassured that we are succeeding in providing the most stick-able and compelling learning experiences. It is critical to provide an adequate amount of time to allow this to happen, with only very measured teacher intervention.

Listening to these learner-led conversations is one of the most significant activities we can undertake. It is also one of the most satisfying and enjoyable aspects of our job. After all, when we start a new topic, meet a new group or create a new learning opportunity, we hope that learners will be so enthused and immersed in their learning that they will take up the reins and lead it forward themselves. When learners are *doing the learning for themselves*, we will know that we have established an outstanding learning climate. When we hear them talking about the lesson after they've walked out the door, we know that they've really started to lead their own learning.

By injecting our own expertise (through questioning, coaching and clarification strategies) into peer-led learning conversations, we can take the best elements of the informal learning interactions you might overhear at your local skate-park and come up with a truly engaging learning experience. Our role as teacher is as an expert pedagogue, creating lessons that are rich in the language of feedback and continuous on-going assessment.

You are an expert pedagogue because …

You have an astute awareness of *when* and *how* to intervene.

Your timing for interventions and coaching conversations is determined by what you hear, see and sense (informed by your well-honed professional intuition).

You employ a range of strategies to observe and gather learning intelligence – such as asking powerful questions, using a learning wall for feedback, sticky notes placed on tables where groups are working and digital photographs and audio/software packages that allow you to collate and reflect back to the group what you see.

You agree clear criteria with the group for any interventions you will make (e.g. to correct inaccuracies/misconceptions, to respond to a learning-focused question).

You use assessment criteria to communicate clear expectations that learners need to share their thinking with each other.

You maintain a delicate balance between expert-coach and expert-interventionist.

You have the confidence to stand back, be quiet and let the learning happen.

Your language, actions and physical environment value the process of learning alongside the product and includes explicit questions to promote the development of effective learning dispositions.

You have a well-developed sense of timing for any interventions you decide to make.

You provide specific opportunities within the session to reflect and celebrate learners' progress back to them, informed by your intelligence gathering.

Your interventions are, first and foremost, informed by the feedback you receive *ahead* of the feedback you then provide.

You design learning opportunities that explicitly demand independent learning.

You actively seek out opportunities to listen to learning talk during tasks.

You engage in forensic questioning to check out the security of knowledge, understanding and skills.

You provide specific opportunities within the session to require learners to reflect on the progress they are making and identify the next steps they need to take.

Feedback channel 2: Learner to teacher

It is by listening to what the students say, watching how they respond and capturing the breakthrough moments within their conversations that we can provide them with a true sense of their progression. One way of looking at the learning process might be as a progression diagram (see page 177).

In some subjects, the challenge to develop discussion and creative thinking can be difficult, not least because many learners hem themselves in by the perception that certain subjects are all about two answers: right and wrong. As a result, they often lack the necessary confidence to think freely, discuss and suggest a *range* of possibilities. One way to encourage greater self-confidence is to increase the amount of '{insert subject here} talk' in lessons. The idea is that if learners are given regular and varied opportunities to articulate their thinking, they are also being given permission to get things wrong and present alternative approaches and solutions. An integral part of this process is the opportunity for high quality two-way feedback. By planning lessons that contain *dedicated* times for learning talk you can have a really positive effect. A welcome by-product of learning talk is that when *they* are talking, you will be listening. This will enable you to build *your* learning intelligence as an expert pedagogue.

Grow the gap

Whenever we pose questions, tasks or problems to our learners, it's only natural to want to jump into the gap between what we ask and the learners' response. After all, we all want to acknowledge insight, celebrate accuracy and address any misconceptions or inaccuracies as quickly as possible. But it is this gap *between* the question and the response that makes the difference between a dependent, passive learning culture and an independent, actively-thinking learning culture. It's in that precious gap that the learning happens.

Ultimately it is when and how we intervene in the learning process that is critical to the quality of learning talk that follows. When we listen carefully, seek clarification

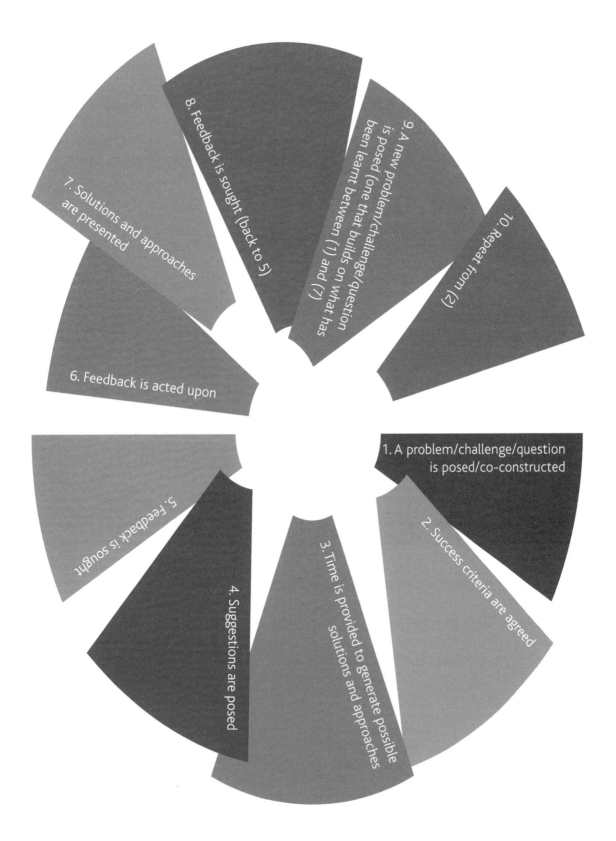

8. Feedback is sought (back to 5)

9. A new problem/challenge/question is posed (one that builds on what has been learnt between (1) and (7)

7. Solutions and approaches are presented

10. Repeat from (2)

6. Feedback is acted upon

5. Feedback is sought

1. A problem/challenge/question is posed/co-constructed

2. Success criteria are agreed

4. Suggestions are posed

3. Time is provided to generate possible solutions and approaches

and ask others to appraise explanations, we'll know that the learning environment is doing its job in fostering an atmosphere of intellectual risk-taking and we will find ourselves in a climate that welcomes open and honest intellectual challenge. Not only that, but if we can get our learners to lead this themselves by modelling it to them, then we're already halfway there.

It is worth noting that because we hold the position of 'knowledgeable adult' or 'leader', in the room, it is *our* responses that, rightly or wrongly, often have the greatest power and influence. But the most important ideas don't actually come from us – they come from our learners. Establishing a culture of intellectual challenge in our lessons will reap delightful benefits to those of us who want to sit back and admire the wealth of learning capacities in every individual. Admittedly, it seems to be a rare group member, particularly in the adult world, who is prepared to challenge the view of the 'leader', yet it is just that exceptional thinking that we want to encourage.

Research[36] suggests that growing the gap in this way can make a significant impact on the quality of learning (thinking, processing, speculating, working out etc.) of learners. Daniel Kahneman[37], a Nobel Prize Winner in Economics (2002) for his work with Amos Tversky on decision-making and uncertainty, enhances this evidence from our classrooms. He explains that we all have two systems of thinking:

System 1: Fast, intuitive and emotional

System 2: Slow, deliberative and logical

Both systems work well together, but there are times when one system is more effective than the other. The key for us is to make sure learners get enough practice at using *both* systems when they are learning. What we know from the classroom and from the research is that there is often a gap of less than one second between the posing of a question and a response. This would suggest that the fast, intuitive and emotional thinking system (System 1) gets a really good work-out during the

---

36 Posted on http://independentthinking.posterous.com/the-power-of-wait-time (2/11/11) by Ian Gilbert from an original paper by Kathleen Cotton 'Classroom Questioning.' North West Regional Educational Laboratory http://educationnorthwest.org/webfm_send/569

37 Kahneman, D., *Thinking, Fast and Slow*, (London: Penguin, 2011).

school day leaving the slow, deliberative and logical system of thinking (System 2) neglected and unloved at the bottom of the metaphorical school bag. If we are to provide learners with opportunities to develop their ability to apply considerate, mindful and logical thinking to the questions we pose, then growing the gap by staying out of it is one powerful way to achieve this.

There are a number of steps that we can take to make the gap count:

 Deliberately plan to leave significant time (the 'gap') *before* we request learners' responses. 'Significant time' is at *least* three seconds, according to recent research into classroom questioning.

 Explain to learners what we are expecting to *hear* and *see* during this time. Make this explicit in learning intentions, outcomes and success criteria.

3 Explicitly assess and feedback on the quality of learning talk that takes place between question and response.

4 *Model* how to use thinking time by:

a Leave deliberate and considered pauses in our own reactions to learners' responses and avoiding the temptation to respond to the first hand up. Use a timer to let the learners get used to learning *in* the gap. Many of us, and learners are no exception, feel uncomfortable in silence, so we need to let everybody know that it is deliberate, not that we've forgotten what we were going to do next. One indicator that quality relationships exist in our lessons is being able to inhabit these gaps comfortably and let the learning happen.

b Work through problems and speak our thoughts *out loud* so the whole group can hear and watch the deliberate, logical system of thinking that we are expecting to happen within the gap. This way, learners are shown exactly what quality thinking-in-action sounds and looks like.

5 Monitor the balance of (1) feedback *given* versus feedback *received* and (2) opportunities for fast, intuitive thinking versus slow, deliberative thinking and make sure there is a balance across a series of lessons. You can set a

target ranging anywhere from approximately 40:60 (given: received) to 20:80 or *even* 15:85, as appropriate. Use the gap that you create to seek feedback by listening and observing your learners thinking deeply.

We know that letting the learners know how well they are doing is a fundamental aspect of effective teaching and learning. If the balance is wrong, the feedback we give may end up drowning out the feedback we need to receive about how learners are working through problems and how we need to adapt in response to them. Not only that, but if we reduce the gap for thinking, we are reducing the number of opportunities to open up the third feedback channel of learner-to-learner feedback. This can lead to over-dependence and passivity on the part of learners who are overwhelmed by too much teacher-talk and know that all they have to do is wait long enough and the solution will be provided for them. With the right balance, however, we can create a gap that is full of quality thinking and processing. In this way, feedback can take its rightful place as an integral part of the drawing out process that lies at the heart of Full On Learning. Getting the balance right is critical.

One way of communicating the importance of a thinking gap to *your learners* might look like an unpicked version of 'Think-Pair-Share':

Clarify success criteria. What are you looking for? What does quality thinking look, sound and feel like for you/them?

Pose the question.

Think Time: Learners to think about and think through (try to wait for *at least* 3 seconds between posing the question and accepting responses, there's more about this later in the chapter).

Process: Learners process the information on their own (happens within the 3 second *minimum* think-time specified above).

Process: Learners check out their responses with each other (*at least* 12 seconds). Additional activities could be incorporated here, e.g. pose a 'What if?' question to refine each others' response, or add at least two more ideas to the original responses, then select the best one.

Formulate: Learners make deliberately considered responses to move thinking on.

This quality gap gives *us* the chance to:

 Assess levels of engagement, security of understanding and confidence to articulate thinking.

Establish the gap for deliberative, logical and DEEP thinking.

Listen to learning conversations and collect feedback.

Gather our learning intelligence taken from (a) and (b) to inform our next move.

Provide specific feedback on the quality of thinking and learning talk.

Ensure teaching is matched and adaptive to learning.

The dual feedback channels of learner-to-teacher and teacher-to-learner can work independently of each other at different points in the lesson or, if you want really powerful learning to make progress visible, you can couple the channels together.

If you want to check that you are on track, you can enlist the help of a fellow teacher, teaching assistant or a student member of the group and ask them to monitor how much teacher-talk in your lessons compared to learner-talk. If done with learners, it can act as a springboard for quality learning conversations about the pace of 'getting through' versus the pace of 'developing understanding'.

Observing learning to gather learning intelligence

A central part of the pedagogy of Early Years Practitioners involves observing children as they explore, discover and test things out for themselves. I was once discussing Early Years Foundation Stage practice with an Ofsted inspector and she ended the conversation with a sigh of resignation and the observation that, 'Every teacher needs to watch an outstanding Early Years Practitioner if they really want to understand how children learn.'

The art of observing learning in order to give quality feedback requires a sharp eye, a keen ear and a packet of sticky notes. From here on, you can develop amazingly sophisticated ways to capture learning:

You can only do this well if the learning opportunities you design encourage *independent* learning opportunities (independent of you, not necessarily of each other).

You need to have a single or at least a *limited* focus for your observation prior to the start of the lesson. This allows you to communicate your learning intentions (your role) and the success criteria for the task to your group from the outset.

If everything goes well you will be fully occupied during this activity. This means that during a collaborative task you will not be intervening and disrupting learners' independent thinking and processing. As such, it supports you in your endeavour to 'let the learning happen'. It also means you won't feel guilty for apparently 'not doing anything'. Observing learning will keep you very busy whilst you are doing it.

Observing learning results in you actively and deliberately undertaking ongoing continuous assessment. This is platinum-standard formative assessment practice.

You are modelling research and enquiry to your learners whilst they complete the challenge you set. This means they get to see you learning about them.

You will be able to provide targeted and immediate feedback through your observations (they can be time-indexed, written on sticky notes and placed by the side of the learner or on a feedback wall to be collected at an appropriate time by learners).

You will have collected a wealth of learning intelligence about how well your learners engage with the challenge you set them, their level of concentration, their ability to work together and a whole host of other incredibly valuable pieces of learning data. All of which can be reflected back to them during your planned reflection sessions during the lesson. This, in turn, makes their progress clearly visible to all in the room.

By engaging students in this activity, you are offering them the opportunity to practise their ability to take responsibility for their own learning and encouraging high expectations of engagement. After all, in return they are going to receive some high quality feedback on what they are doing which in turn will support their progression. If you want to do this, a useful place to start is to provide them with some observation prompts, a template or key questions as a 'script' to work from. This will also help to avoid learners making inappropriate comments before they get accustomed to the process. The section below includes a possible template to adapt and the chapter on questioning contains useful questions that can be used by learners to develop these skills in self- and peer-assessment.

Stop, look and listen

One way of rapidly gathering learning intelligence from a group is inspired by the simple mantra from my childhood of the Green Cross Code: stop, look and listen (SL and L). This method enables you to stop teaching and then take a quick looking and listening 'health check' on what progress is being made and, just as speedily, reflect it back to your group. As soon as you have set up the task, grab your 'SL and L' sheet and make some quick notes. You may want to capture quotes from the group, examples of positive body language or an instance of somebody struggling (i.e. learning). Another benefit is that it allows you to step back, defer any interventions and assess how well the challenge has been understood. If there is confusion, you'll see it quickly and be able to respond appropriately. In this way, you will be allowing *your* learning intelligence to inform your teaching practice.

Observing learning in three steps

For more significant intelligence gathering, you can use the describe–interpret–feedback process outlined below. This is really powerful when you are in a deep learning session, perhaps a piece of project work or a rich challenge designed to draw out independence, creativity and problem-solving. Once again, it allows you to step back, collect intelligence and reflect progress back to the whole group and/or individual learners.

 Describe what you see and hear

The role of teacher-as-observer is, first and foremost, to *describe* what you see. The key is to defer judgement and interpretation. This approach encourages you to make a distinct separation between description and interpretation. First, you describe and *then* you take time, preferably with a coaching partner or with the learners, to reflect on what you have seen before you interpret and assess the quality of learning that has taken place.

Observations and feedback you could offer include:

'You are taking time to listen to each member of the group.'

'Everybody looks excited and keen to get things done.'

'There are a lot of different approaches here.'

'You have generated a number of interesting ideas.'

'There's lots of eye contact with the rest of the group.'

'A detailed plan of action.'

'Everybody is contributing in this group.'

'You have used lots of different resources to come up with your ideas.'

I found observing learning in this way very challenging at first. As teachers, we have highly developed analytical thinking patterns that we rely on every day. We spend so much of our time rapidly interpreting and speculating about the words and behaviour of others, there is a huge temptation to rush to make concrete assertions about the quality of learning. If this happens, it can result in closing down thinking and, more importantly, impeding our ability to pose questions to the learners as part of *their* feedback because *we've* already formed a judgement as to what learning may or may not have happened.

 Use questions to redirect thinking or address inaccuracies

Intervening in a timely fashion, with a pertinent question, can help us to redirect learners' thinking and address any inaccuracies when they occur. (There's more on this in Chapter 9.) These feedback remarks can contain slightly more judgemental language but they should still serve as an excellent way to employ formative assessment. These interventions do provide an interruption but they don't disrupt the whole group or task. For example:

'I like the way you've focused on the first part of the challenge; how will you make sure you leave time to cover everything else you need to do?'

Stop, look and listen checklist

	OBSERVATIONS (What happened? Who was involved?)	TIME (How long for?)	FREQUENCY (How often? How many times?)
STOP			
LOOK			
LISTEN			

'How could you develop the idea of the "expert" a little more?'

'How many alternative ideas have you considered?'

'Is everybody involved in your discussion?'

'When did you last check back with the success criteria?'

'Does everybody understand what they need to do next?'

 Share what you see and hear

There are a number of ways to share feedback in a descriptive and formative way. The ideas below are by no means exhaustive as you will constantly develop new ways once you start using this approach.

Feedback wall

Providing feedback on a 'feedback wall' in the classroom works really well. The learning challenge has to be designed in such a way that all learners can immerse themselves in the task that in turn allows you to circulate. Make a note of relevant body language and group dynamics and listen in so you can capture quotes and questions made by individual learners. By placing the feedback on the wall and away from the main activity the learners are left to focus on the task and only when appropriate will they send a member of the group to collect the feedback from the wall. This can then be shared within the group and used to inform their next steps.

Covert feedback

At a recent gifted and talented conference I lead a workshop during which I shared the 'observing learning' technique, using sticky notes to provide unobtrusive feedback. Following the session, I attended a workshop being delivered by a colleague. As I sat down, she swooped in and placed a sticky note in front of me that said, 'Thank you for coming to my session'. Apart from it being lovely that she had adapted something I had suggested earlier in my workshop, it was fascinating to be on the receiving end of this technique. It really did have the effect of making me feel *personally* welcomed into the session, more so than the generic greeting that was offered to the whole group. One of the next notes our table received came just after we had been discussing whether an 'expert' would be needed to help us with the problem at hand. As if by magic, a yellow note appeared on our table, 'Explore the idea of the role of the expert a little more'. My partner and I, who had only just met, willingly took this direction and, rather than moving on through the task as we had planned to do, we started digging deeper into the challenge and had an involved discussion about the role of experts. We were then asked to join with the others on our table and share our ideas.

The striking thing about this was that although the rest of the table had approached the challenge in a very similar way, they had only scratched the surface of the role of the expert, and had moved on to the last stages of the problem, just as we had originally planned to do. Our response to the problem, when compared with the rest of our group, was deeper, had many more connections and, to be honest, was far more insightful. All of this was entirely because of the sticky note intervention. It had the effect of applying a brake on our thinking – we had been given the teacher's permission to go deeper rather than go on. It wasn't until then that I really understood the full power of the strategy.

Learner-to-learner feedback

Students can use observation strategies for themselves. A good place to start with this is to provide the learners with a template like the 'Stop, Look and Listen' example provided, script of questions (there's a collection of reflective questions in the chapter all about questioning) or simply to identify '3 things to look and listen out for', and make a note of it when it happens. This helps to encourage learners to make very specific observations against agreed success criteria and can help to avoid inappropriate comments at the same time. Increasing our self-awareness will prompt change and change is, after all, a pretty good way of defining what we mean by 'learning'. If I am to learn anything, I need to know where I am, where I need to be and what I need to do to get there. Observing learning-in-action is a great way to learn from alternative approaches, false-starts and successes. A high level of self-awareness can then come about as a part of a dialogue between learners and those around them, whether teacher, a coach or peer learner.

Documenting learning

Seeing and recording learning moments is critical to capturing key moments of progression and in developing a shared language of learning. It enables us to articulate what we have done well so that we can repeat it and what we need to do to improve. If learners are to develop discernment, we need to design opportunities for them to practise offering observations and reflections in their on- and off-line contributions. The access and availability of video and audio to document learning provides us with a fantastic opportunity to develop digital confidence and literacy for our learners and for ourselves as practitioners. But a learning log or scrapbook of observations serves a similar purpose. Using very low-tech approaches (photographs, video cameras, sticky notes on a timeline) enables us to record a baseline of prior expectations and then document learning goals and key milestones along the way.

Digital feedback

The ability to give and receive feedback will be fundamental not only to the individual's level of involvement in wider society but also to the quality of the society they become a part of. One of the reasons that YouTube is blocked in many schools is not because of its content per se, but because of the inappropriate comments you may find logged beneath a video. This is a real issue if we are going to encourage young people to engage positively (as contributors and participants) with the online world. They should know how to craft appropriate comments for themselves and how to flag those that are inappropriate. The skill of the moderator will be in high demand in the 21st century learner's repertoire and, as such, we need to design learning that provides opportunities for mindful practice from the moment children and young people are able to switch on their computer or smartphone.

DESCRIBE Write down *only* what you observe	INTERPRET Impact this has on knowledge building		FEEDBACK How you share this with learners
What you hear	+	-	
What you see	+	-	
Interactions within the group	+	-	

The thinking culture

It is worth involving your learners in a discussion about what 'thinking culture' would look, sound and feel like. This activity can also act as a prompt to reflect on the role and responsibilities of the learner and the teacher in a high-quality thinking environment. For example, what is *their* role in maintaining a quality climate for thinking? What learning behaviours do *they/you* need to display? How much time, in total, do you *all* need in order to formulate responses, share initial ideas and propose suggestions?

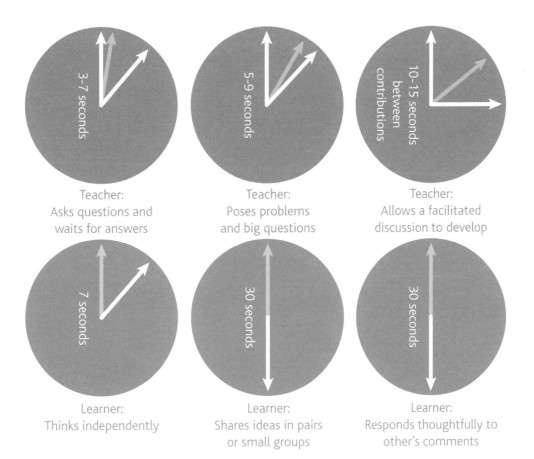

Teacher:
Asks questions and
waits for answers

Teacher:
Poses problems
and big questions

Teacher:
Allows a facilitated
discussion to develop

Learner:
Thinks independently

Learner:
Shares ideas in pairs
or small groups

Learner:
Responds thoughtfully to
other's comments

Action Research

How can I create a shared and authentic learning dialogue with students?

How do I know that they've 'got it'?

What does a 'climate for thinking' look, sound and feel like?

How can I show progress in learning (make learning visible) at any stage of the lesson?

How can I communicate the progress that learners are making back to them, as it happens?

How can I assess and adapt my teaching to respond to misconceptions?

How can I encourage learners to use their own misunderstandings to direct their next steps?

What practical tools are available to support quality feedback and self-reflection?

How can I establish a confident and reflective learning community in my lessons?

How can I enhance learning relationships through quality feedback?

How can I stand back to capture and report back when I 'let the learning happen'?

dependent on effort

Yoda and Sophocles in conversation

Success is

| | LEARNERS WHO ... | TEACHING THAT ... |

LEARNERS WHO ...	TEACHING THAT ...
Ensure learning is personal to them. Are able to draw on experiences from the wider world, beyond the classroom and the school to enhance their personal development	Makes it safe and appropriate for learners to refer to and share their own experiences, objects of importance and memories
Are able to make informed choices about what, how, who with and when they are going to learn	Offers opportunities for learners to co-designs tasks, projects and activities. Holds the learners to account according to agreed success criteria
Are confident in presenting ideas, thoughts and learning with peers and wider audiences. Respond actively and positively to feedback	Enables frequent and varied opportunities for learners to present their learning – both outcome and process. Classroom displays show that the process of learning is valued (e.g. drafts, amendments, changes, adaptations). Presentations of learning are regular occurrences, with the whole school and wider community invited in to celebrate learning

POWERFUL LEARNERS

Powerful learning projects

Learning is personal. As we discussed earlier, when we know *why* we are doing something, we value it, connect it to other aspects of our lives and engage with it on an individual level. When we practise a skill, we need to know *how* it fits into the bigger picture of our lives. Learning opportunities must make these links explicit and be designed around real-life situations and/or linked to the bigger picture of *why* learning particular subject is important.

There are many project-based learning models[38] that provide helpful frameworks for designing contextual learning opportunities that are relevant. This doesn't mean that we have to redesign the maths curriculum to incorporate the latest popular music craze or make links to the most popular celebrity to bring relevance to geography. Contextual learning enables learners to make sense and meaning *for themselves* of the challenges and questions we pose for them and that they construct for themselves. Taken further, it means we can allow learners to shape their learning *according to their own passions and interests*.

---

38 The innovation unit has a number of useful resources and research that provide such guidelines and frameworks you might find useful; for example: http://www.innovationunit.org/sites/default/files/Teacher's%20Guide%20 to%20Project-based%20Learning.pdf

One such project uses an archaeological approach[39] (for more on this see Chapter 9) in which students are asked to bring in objects of their own choosing and be prepared to explain why they have chosen it and in what ways it is linked to the subject or topic. In the next lesson, the teacher first establishes a safe community of enquiry spending time with the group to consider what an excellent enquiry would look, sound and feel like. The students then place their personally selected objects on the table. One by one they explain what their object is and why it is meaningful to them or, alternatively, how they think it is linked to the topic or subject. The safe learning that has been established allows this to be a deeply revelatory session, which in turn serves to strengthen the learning community.

After the individual revelations, the students are asked to come up with some questions about each other's objects. They write down their questions and place these next to each item. They then go back to their own object and start to consider the questions they have been posed as the first piece of research for their projects. They are given a timeframe of, for example, one week to design their enquiry projects and develop a project brief for themselves that they will work to over the following few lessons. From one personal object, through a safe collaborative social learning activity and a self-designed enquiry project, the learners have an opportunity to produce remarkable and, for the most part, relevant and personal research projects by the end of the agreed timeline.

Powerful learning experiences incorporate a number of factors:

1. **Co-constructed and clear success criteria.** This can be discussed and agreed upon by the group, thereby encouraging learners to get directly involved in their learning and, in doing so, taking responsibility for it. Although it is the teacher's responsibility to set learning objectives and communicate the 'why', 'how' and 'what' of learning, the success criteria for how these objectives will be met can be discussed with the learners. In this way, when it comes to self- and peer-assessment, everybody is clear on what to assess their learning against.

---

39 I first came across an approach like this when I attended a seminar at the University of Bristol Graduate School of Education as part of the ELLI ('Effective Lifelong Learning Inventory') seminar programme in 2008. You can find out more about the ELLI programme at http://www.vitalpartnerships.com/learning-power/

2

Autonomy. Real choices within learning make for a powerful learning experience. If you've already negotiated the success criteria, you have will have given learners permission to think and make choices for themselves and against which they will be assessed. Additional decisions can be made about who they work with, how long they have for the task and in what format their final product will be presented. The key to offering autonomy in this way is to do so by degrees. It can often be more challenging to accept new freedoms and responsibilities than it is to give them. This provides a framework within which independent learning and freedom can be experienced without it feeling like chaos to you or your group.

3

Challenge is integral. But it needn't all be about intellectual challenge. It can also come from the *way* in which we ask them to learn. For some learners, being asked to make decisions about the format of the final piece and who to work with may well present the biggest challenge. For others, it may be in having to collaborate on a task that they think they could do completely on their own. One way to assess what the challenging element will be for them personally is to use a simple self-assessment tool like the one below. Learners who use this or similar ways of identifying levels and types of challenge, feedback that they really like the way in which it allows them to reflect, set *some* goals for themselves (rather than the teacher setting them) and think longer-term about what they might aim for as a result of the project or piece of work they are doing. They also like the visual representation of their progress and some have even shared it with their parents/carers to explain what they're doing in school, which can't be bad.

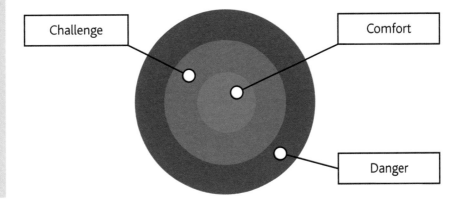

Audience. Ways to validate what has been achieved need to be explicit and public. This means providing an audience to whom the learning will be presented. Consider creating a wider audience than just the peer group. Upping the stakes by inviting in a 'panel of experts' from the parent body, local businesses or simply other teachers to hear the students' efforts is a great way to integrate high levels of challenge and expectation, and make the deadlines very real indeed.

Asking teachers from your cluster or your local area can work really well, particularly if you develop cross-phase shared learning opportunities. Seeking stronger connections between primary and secondary teachers does wonders for learners' self-esteem (whether older or younger children). The opportunity for older learners to model effective learning to their younger peers and vice versa is another way to infect the community with a powerful learning bug. The 'panel of experts' simply need to consist of anybody who has not been directly involved with the particular project.

During the presentations, the teams can be asked to field challenging questions from their peers about the decisions they made, the difficulties they encountered and what they have learnt as a result. The emphasis is on articulating their thinking and ideas and making explicit connections to prior and present learning. In doing this, their learning has both a personal and a wider social context. They are held to account to themselves as they provide a rationale for their actions and reflect on their learning process, and to the wider community of their school and the network of schools. They have to be able to articulate the connections between the decisions they made, the progress of their project and the impact this has had on themselves and their school community. Without the requirement for audience, the power of their learning experiences would be significantly reduced.

Quality end product. With all of the focus on process over product, it would be misleading to think that an end product wasn't necessary. Certainly, some extreme versions of process-focused learning discussed in other parts of this book are praiseworthy and there is a place for them. If we are asking learners to make connections between prior and present learning – to link the periodic table with the Treaty of Versailles, for example – there has to be a final, tangible product that they can point to and say, 'And this is what we came up with'.

Thinking frameworks for powerful learning design

When we want students to learn something, we are actually requiring them to cover three significant 'learning bases' before they get to score the home run (or 'rounder' if, like me, you were brought up on summer sports in the UK). This is a hybrid of the principles of Bloom's and the Triple Whammy Planning question mentioned earlier and how they can be used to inform learning objectives:

1st Base (Cognitive): our ability to make sense of information

Learning objective: What you need to know and understand

2nd Base (Psychomotor): our ability to employ physical skill

Learning objective: What you need to be able to do

3rd Base (Affective): our attitudes and how we feel as a result of what we experience

Learning objective: What you need to be like

Bloom's Revised Taxonomy is often presented as a hierarchy or ladder of increasingly complex thinking functions. This seems to imply that you can't achieve one level of thinking without completing the level below. I've never been convinced that this is the case and practical experience in the classroom would indicate that we do not think in such a regimented way. Often, we might begin with speculation, and then require some factual information (remembering prior learning and using our acquired understanding) to give meaning to our hypothesis. A more fluid representation of Bloom's might look a little like the diagram below. You can adapt this as an observation tool if you want to explore what type of thinking is happening by adding arrows to indicate the interrelationship of the different types of thinking during a discussion.

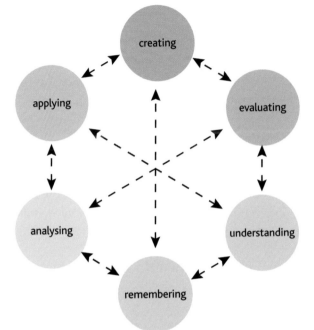

In this way, thinking skills can be interpreted as our 'thinking bases'. They could be colour-coded and organised into clusters, ensuring that you touch a base of each colour as you construct questions. To get learners really involved in this, you can create 'thinking' and 'question' posts around the room and ask learners to stand by particular posts when they are thinking or asking questions at a particular level. Making this categorisation of thinking explicit to students is a valuable way to get them thinking about what is meant by 'quality thinking' and 'quality questions'. Cards or dice with the characteristics of 'quality thinking' printed on them will also encourage students to think at a particular 'level'. It is also a practical way to incorporate a thinking language into the culture of the lesson.

This is a useful way to ensure that it is questions that drive learning, and that we are not inadvertently putting a ceiling on thinking in the tasks we set. By using these thinking bases as a way to organise groups, you can also ask learners to focus on activities and questions according to the base at which you ask them to sit, and then rotate them around the room. This is a great way to differentiate; it allows for surprises as every learner can try all the bases (similar to using de Bono's Thinking Hats in a group discussion). Operating in this way also fosters high aspirations and reinforces a 'have a go' (safe) collaborative culture.

You can also incorporate high levels of autonomy by asking learners to choose at which four bases they want to learn during the lesson. If you ask them to set themselves learning tasks which will find them learning once in their 'comfort zone', twice in their 'challenge zone' and once in their 'danger zone', this will inform their choice as to what thinking challenge they will address.

One example of designing a learning topic through questions and higher order thinking is illustrated below. This is a history example, but the tool can be applied to many subjects and/or topics. In addition to designing learning to address cognitive development (what learners need to know and understand), this tool addresses what learners need to be able to do (psychomotor/skill) and what they need to be like (affective/dispositions).

Creating	Designing, constructing, planning, producing, inventing	Rewrite the Treaty of Versailles so that it reflects fair and equitable justice for all
Evaluating	Checking, hypothesising, critiquing, judging, testing	'The harsh nature of the Treaty of Versailles justifies the rise of German nationalism'. Agree/Disagree
Analysing	Comparing, organising, deconstructing, attributing	Explain which country gained the most out of the Treaty of Versailles
Applying	Implementing, carrying out, using, executing	Write an account of a negotiator taking part in the Treaty of Versailles
Understanding	Interpreting, inferring, summarising, paraphrasing	Show the changes in quality of life and national boundaries as a result of the Treaty of Versailles
Remembering	Recognising, listing, locating, retrieving	List five reasons for the outbreak of the First World War

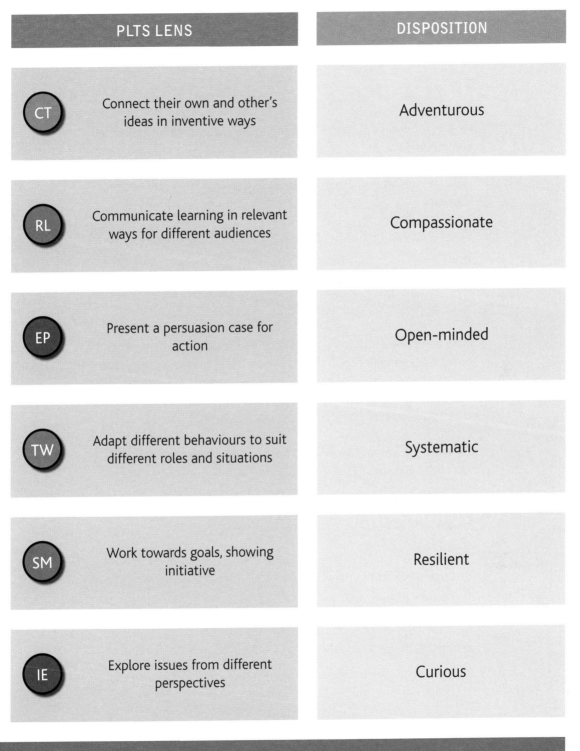

PLTS LENS	DISPOSITION
CT Connect their own and other's ideas in inventive ways	Adventurous
RL Communicate learning in relevant ways for different audiences	Compassionate
EP Present a persuasion case for action	Open-minded
TW Adapt different behaviours to suit different roles and situations	Systematic
SM Work towards goals, showing initiative	Resilient
IE Explore issues from different perspectives	Curious

EXAMPLE: HISTORY

Action research

How can I design powerful learning experiences within the formal curriculum?

How can I establish a regular 'panel of experts' as an audience for learners?

What links can I make between curriculum content and real-world context?

How do I integrate the key ingredients of powerful learning in the learning projects that I design?

How can I tweak what we already do to include some elements of powerful learning? (e.g. a maths lesson that finishes with a presentation of to an expert panel of external observers; a musical event project-managed by learners as a result of cross-curricular collaboration; a cross-generational community project in art etc.)

How can I develop learner-confidence to co-design success-criteria and learning outcomes?

How can I encourage learner-networking through my design of power-ful learning projects?

What local, regional or international connections could I develop through physical or virtual contact to enhance the power of specific curriculum areas?

In what ways do I need to adapt my teaching to create space for auton-omous learning? With whom can I work alongside to develop this?

In what ways can I assess very distinctive and varied projects against shared criteria?

Focus on

 Making it real – blurring the formal and informal learning lines/providing authentic context.

 Explicitly involving learners in the design, structure and delivery of the project.

 Creating networks of learning teams, each taking responsibility for their individual project plan.

 Allowing projects to look, feel and sound different according to each team's plan.

 Acting as coach rather than leader.

Make sure the learning teams know what a quality outcome will look, sound and feel like for them and that they have frequent opportunities to reflect on their progress.

us

from

the most important

... they come from our learners

come

don't

LEARNERS WHO ...	TEACHING THAT ...
Choose to commit their time and effort to investigating aspects of their learning that they enjoy and find interesting and challenging, because they are driven by curiosity about the world in which they live	Designs learning challenges that are peppered with questions and provide deliberate opportunities for discussion, debate and investigation
Thrive when faced with unfamiliar ideas, objects and challenges. Actively engage in discussions, debate through listening and contributing ideas, reflecting on own and other's contributions and summarising pertinent points in discussions	Establishes an environment of curiosity. Embraces new technologies, artefacts and objects as part of an exploratory of learning. Employs anticipation as an effective part of building excitement in learning
Ask quality questions that reflect highest order thinking (speculation, hypothesising and knowledge-creation) and can structure their own enquiry routes	Designs thinking and enquiry frameworks to support independent learner enquiry and promote investigative thinking. Develops agreed success criteria with learners to assess the quality of questions posed

- - -→ # QUESTIONING

One of the best ways for learners to participate - physically and mentally that is - in the lesson is through the questions they pose and answer. This ensures that learning is an active, engaging and thoroughly involved process. In asking questions, we are genuinely saying, 'I want to know what *you* think because what *you* think matters'. It gives a message to the whole group that the learning belongs to the students, not the teacher. Another way of putting it, 'It is *your* duty to be curious'.[40] Not a bad slogan to have over your classroom door.

The power of questions

In posing quality questions, we encourage learners to provide responses that require them to practise using their higher order thinking. Great questions inspire more questions. In the same way, great questioning results in learners speculating and hypothesising and developing their thinking as they construct their own questions. Effective learning is characterised by a question-rich climate where learners feel safe and confident enough to generate a diverse range of possible solutions and ideas.

As teachers, we can use our instinctive questioning skills to tease out knowledge, clarify thinking and address misconceptions. Through persistent questioning, learners can pose solutions to challenges and problems. More to the point, they

---

40 Lucy Sweetman http://lucysweetman.thirdsector.co.uk/2012/04/30/we-have-a-duty-to-be-curious/

will quickly learn to deploy their questions with missile-like accuracy to stimulate discussion, debate and thinking.

As we have already seen, in a world flooded with information, the ability to be discerning is vital. Learners need to be able to select information appropriate for their purpose and their audience; to make decisions about what constitutes quality information and whether it originates from a reliable source. All of this requires a highly developed ability to pose thoughtful questions and challenge given information. Discerning thinkers may well inherit the earth or, at the very least, dominate the digital information landscape.

Questioning is the life-blood of Full On Learning. It is the most frequent way in which teachers and pupils interact, so the trick is to really make it count. It is also one of the key influencers on the progress made by each pupil, and it is the most immediate and accessible way for teachers to identify how much learning is going on. The most skilful practitioners I have observed have all had a knack of asking questions just at the right moment, rather than giving answers. These teachers are relentless in drawing out learning through their questions and squeezing every last drop of thinking from the topic. They also employ a disciplined approach to their questioning in how they grow the thinking gap by using wait time (explained in detail in Chapter 8).

The great thing about questioning is that it can be deliberately practised and developed. John Hattie in his famous 'meta-research' refers to it as one of the most intrusive acts of teaching. For him, questioning doesn't represent the *greatest* influence on student learning but, with an effect size of 0.4, it does represent one of the strongest influences on student learning.[41]

---

41 John Hattie *Visible Learning* pp.192-193 'Self-verbalization and self-questioning' and his website at http:// education/auckland.ac.nz/home/about/staff/j.hattie

Questions as a learning lens

One of the ways in which I have improved my range of questioning strategies is by asking colleagues and students to listen to my own questioning at different stages during a lesson. I started to do this after I noticed that the majority of meaty discussion in my lessons only really took place towards the end of the lesson. This raised two issues for me. First, it meant that we often ran out of time to delve deeply into the topic under discussion. This, in turn, resulted in a fairly weak final plenary, if there was time for one at all (oh, the shame!). Second, and of equal concern, was that if the discussion and questioning was only happening at the end of the lesson, the rest of the lesson must, by implication, have been led by me and dominated by teacher-talk rather than student-talk. So something had to change.

It has *always* been my firm belief that students learn best when they are involved in the construction of enquiry, but this revelation about my questioning made this pretty impossible. If the active involvement of learners only came about as a result of *me* controlling and giving them permission to get involved, then I was missing a huge learning opportunity.

One tool that helped me then and that I continue to use is the 'Observing Questions' capture sheet below. It works by dividing the lesson into phases (you decide how you want to break up the lesson) to assess the quality of questions being asked by the teacher. The observer simply keeps a tally chart of the type of question being asked in each phase of the lesson. The specific *type* of question that you might want to look for is entirely up to you. You can also design a similar format that identifies *who* asks the questions. This example is designed to capture the quantity of questions of a particular type being asked by the teacher during the phases of a lesson.

Once the lesson has been observed, you can turn the tally chart into a graph that will form the basis of a coaching discussion on how effective your questioning was. This is especially useful to compare what you *intended* to happen, what you *thought* happened (the two great coaching questions) and what *actually* happened (the feedback crunch!). The example below shows that *sequences* of questions (where one question was followed up with others to demand extended answers

213

OBSERVING QUESTIONS TEMPLATE					
TYPE OF QUESTION:	PHASE 1	PHASE 2	PHASE 3	PHASE 4	NOTES
Closed questions: *When there is an expected/specific answer – factual recall*					
Open questions: *When there are a variety of possible answers – thinking skills*					
Lower order questions: *When pupils are required to describe, relate, identify, etc. – no development is expected*					

TYPE OF QUESTION:	PHASE 1	PHASE 2	PHASE 3	PHASE 4	NOTES
OBSERVING QUESTIONS TEMPLATE					
Higher order questions: *When pupils are required to analyse, relate, compare, evaluate, justify, etc. – further development is expected*					
Control questions: *Concerned with behaviour for learning*					
Sequences of questions: *When questions build or link to pupil responses and gradually demand higher order thinking skills*					

and, therefore, deeper thinking) only happened in the first phase of the lesson. The lesson end was characterised by closed and lower order questions. In a post-lesson coaching conversation, you can ask questions like, 'What do you see here?' 'What patterns emerge?' And 'In what ways does this map against what you intended to happen?' and so on. It is worth noting that one lesson alone provides a very limited snapshot. This method of observing is designed for development and cannot be used to make judgements. As such, it can be used in a number of lessons to build a picture of pedagogy over time as part of an individual coaching programme. It can also be used to create a picture of the style of questioning across a learning stage or department and provoke great learning conversations.

(NB Nowadays, what you have created falls into the realm of 'infographics' and you can encourage learners to make their own infographics as part of communicating complex information. There's a rapidly growing number of online tools to create your own infographics – have a Google and see what you find).

You can use any thinking framework to inform directly your question-focused lesson planning so lessons can be planned through questions rather than content. Alongside being clear about what your learners will cover and learn about, you'll identify and involve them in the 'big' questions relating to each topic. In this way, you can be clear about what you want them to think about during the lesson and your questioning can become a powerful assessment lens through which to make their thinking visible to them and you.

Student reflection on quality questions

To draw out the learners' ability to pose their *own* quality questions, you can give two group members (two provides safety as they are going to be put on the spot as 'experts') some detailed information about a topic. They become the 'experts' on this topic. In groups, the students must act as interrogators to discover as much information about the topic as possible but restrict them by allowing them to pose *only three quality* questions (they need to be discerning and creative here).

Questioning Data Analysis Example

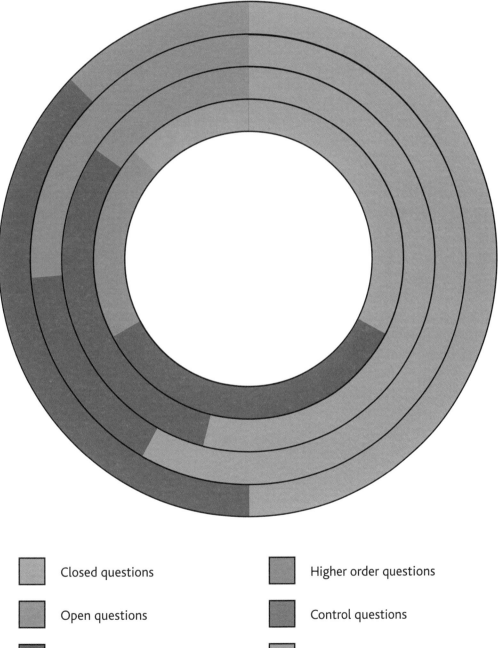

Closed questions

Open questions

Lower order questions

Higher order questions

Control questions

Sequences of questions

Give them time to prepare their questions (they can use a framework or some question-prompts as a script) and ensure the success criteria includes 'Ask questions that will elicit the most information from their "expert"' At the end of the enquiry, the groups collate their information to assess the quality of information they managed to extract. The plenary asks all students to consider not only the quality and amount of information they acquired, but also what their 'best' questions were and why, and what would have been a 'better' question for next time.

You can then break this down into sub-questions to identify what exactly (a) *you* want students to understand (b) they think they need to understand as a result of being in your company for the lesson. A beneficial side-effect is that you will also develop a far more robust approach to assessment. Once you design learning opportunities through questioning, you can then focus on sharpening your own questioning skills that extract the best thinking, identify inaccuracies and assess the security of the learning. This will clarify progression for both you and the learners.

Very soon you are likely to develop a reputation for relentlessly asking your students to elaborate on their thinking. You'll be accused of 'bugging' them so that they can never get away with giving anything less than a full answer. They'll know that a single-word response just won't do. If this is the case, then you'll know that at least with this part of the battle of teaching and learning, you'll have achieved a significant victory.

Learner questions and 'idea-generation'

Asking students to generate their own questions acts as a great way to discuss 'What makes a quality question?' and can lead into joint thinking using assessment grading and/or levelling systems. A little bit of game-playing (variations on '20 questions'; hot-seating; interviewing; creating investigative podcasts; role-playing; responding to information with 'what else?' or 'why?' or 'then what?' and so on) also helps to promote better questioning and, therefore, deeper thinking.

Archaeological enquiry

Use artefacts/objects/diagrams/audio clips etc.

Ask students to build a **sequence of questions**: What? How? When? Why? What if? Who? How is it used? Who does it belong to? Why's it important? What do I think? What do others think? Why does this matter? etc.

Questions are **underpinned by 'learning-skills' questions**: how will you find out? Who can you ask? etc.

The archaeological enquiry technique encourages learners to make links between their personal experiences and the topic being explored. Starting with an object and asking 'Who knows anything about this?' is an open-ended lead-in to discussion followed by 'What do you think we need to know about this?' It assesses prior knowledge, promotes open-ended thinking and explicitly fosters curiosity. From this point, learners can develop a string of questions they think will help them, as a group, to find out more. Using artefacts in this way means that we can ask learners to come up with as many different ideas about what it may have been used for, when and by whom, or just get them to make links with the topic for the lesson. There may well be a definitive 'right' answer, for the original function of the artefact, but to get there, learners have to be prompted to *think* and generate ideas and propose possibilities. Some suggestions from learners may even be seen as being a better idea than the original 'correct' use of the artefact. Furthermore, ideas generation is a characteristic of creative thinking and encourages higher order thinking. In addition, starting with an object, picture, or piece of music provides a level playing field for learners because you are presenting it as 'new'. This means that there really are no right or wrong answers, at this questioning and thinking-stage, just ideas and possibilities.

I don't know whether questioning is the *most* powerful thing that teachers can do to progress the thinking of learners, (I have a suspicion it might be) but it must surely come into our top five. Questioning is the reassuring hand we can hold out

PURPOSE	BENEFIT	EXAMPLE
Focusing thinking	There is strong social pressure to answer any question. Questions can be a useful learning-focus tool to grab attention and keep the learning moving forward. And we all know that our names are the most powerful words to us, so using them to ask questions works very effectively	'Billy, what ideas have your group come up with?' 'Gemma, please would you have a go at responding to the next section of the text?'
Assess understanding, clarification and consolidation	These are the bread and butter of learning. Questions designed to extract information, put together the bigger picture or to enhance understanding	'What, why, how, when, how much ...'
Address misconceptions and inaccuracies. Promote quality learning conversations	As a coach, you can assess as you ask. Questions designed to swing the balance of talk from you to the learner enable you to address any misconceptions and inaccuracies. Similarly, using these types of questions encourages meta-cognition	'That's an interesting approach, John. How did you come to that conclusion?' 'How did it feel to work in this way?'
Building learning communities and making it safe to have a go and contribute	Simply asking questions strengthens the relationship between teacher and student because you are inviting them to lead the conversation. All too often, these questions are the first casualties of the frenetic pace of school life	Anything from 'How are you this morning, Jane?' to a fully structured meet and greet session to build learning communities at the beginning of the week will enhance the safe environment of learning

Flip-thinking: answering questions with questions, posing speculative questions in response to ideas

This is a sneaky way of modelling higher order thinking for students. A simple speculative question encourages further discussion and demonstrates how responding through questions can expand the discussion

Simply asking 'What if …?' or 'What happens next?' or 'What came before?' should do the trick.

To develop deeper thinking, promoting confidence in learners to challenge knowledge and established ways of thinking, and test it out

Rhetorical questions can be used to invite students to really consider what you or others are saying. This is a useful way to develop debates and discussions. Using deliberate inaccuracies invites students to make their own corrections and explain why they think you are wrong

'Does a triangle have four sides?'

'What else could we deduce from this?'

To encourage elaboration of thinking – demanding more than just a single response, with an illustration/ example/ comparison

Inviting students to explain their thinking in more detail. This allows you to make a quick assessment of the security of understanding of the student *and* encourages students to articulate their thinking so they consolidate their learning

'Would you say a bit more about that, and use an example, so that we can get a clearer idea of what you are thinking?'

'Yes, but how would you then link that to …?'

'Did everybody understand how Jessica's group got that answer? Would you show us your working out?'

to learners as we say, 'C'mon, jump in and get involved'. The questions posed by practitioners should be deployed in the same way that a surgeon makes her first incision or a sculptor moulds his clay. Questioning is the nuts and bolts of Full On Learning architecture.

The great thing about questioning is that everybody can get involved – learners and teachers alike. As such, it becomes the essence of collaborative discovery and the co-construction of knowledge and understanding. The table on pages 220-221 offers just some suggestions for ways to develop questioning repertoire. There are many more in use in our lessons every day. Just listen out for them.

If there is just one piece of evidence that I can use to support the Full On premise that the skill of teaching is a deliberately learned act, it is the skill of questioning. Just as we can get better at organising group work, leading learning conversations or using technological tools to enhance learning, we can get better at questioning. And so can our students. In this way, we can all, students and teachers alike, get better at learning. But to do so, we need to deliberately and mindfully practise it.

There's no such thing as a stupid question, just one that could be improved, opened out or deepened. The sharper our questioning, the deeper it will probe thinking and the more information it will draw out. When it comes to questioning, what you put in definitely defines what you get out. Different types of question allow us to chivvy and chase learning around the room, in and out of learners' brains, enabling them to glue together individual pieces of understanding.

Planned questions

Although you could argue that *all* questions should be planned, there are *some* that represent the 'biggies' in any topic. This is about identifying the most important questions that you want students to be able to answer by the end of the topic or lesson.

When exploring the causes of the Second World War, there are some huge questions that we would all ask historians to answer, 'In what ways does war solve problems?' 'War is never the "last resort" – in what ways do you agree or disagree?' When we limit ourselves to posing topic-specific or subject-specific questions, we give students the impression that teaching and learning is simply a question of answering very specific but limited questions. It can also leave learners with the impression that there is simply a right or a wrong answer – so what's the point of discussing it? If, on the other hand, we anchor the subject-specific question in the huge question of - returning to the Second World War example - 'In what ways could it be said that war is inevitable?', we communicate to learners that history, as a lens through which to view the world, is a powerful and extremely relevant way of thinking about the world we live in *now* as well as understanding what has happened before.

Planned	Identify the MOST important questions you want ALL students to be able to answer by the end of the lesson

Topic: Causes of the Second World War	**Huge Question** What can history teach us about the inevitability of war?
	Big Specific Question Explain what you consider to be the most significant events in the lead-up to World War 2 between 1929 and 1939
	Sub-Specific Question How did these events affect how the 'everyday' German people felt about their country?

Sequential questions

Stringing questions together encourages learners to make links between ideas, facts and concepts. By identifying the potential links in a question chain ahead of posing them to learners, you are ready to both demand and anticipate deeper thinking. A simple method might be to design learning around the Five Ws, a tried and tested method of encouraging deeper, connected thinking in response to a topic. Apply this to any subject area and you will find discussion and learning talk increases. Apply it to connected curriculum areas, like the examples below, and learners will find their brains twisting and turning to extract meaning, make connections, deepen their understanding and create new knowledge.

Try applying the Five Ws to the following cross-curricular questions:

Design Technology and the geography of the way in which Mount St Helens erupted

Mathematics and Beethoven's Moonlight Sonata

Science and the building of a Hindu temple

Sequential	Make links between questions so that they become the building blocks of learning

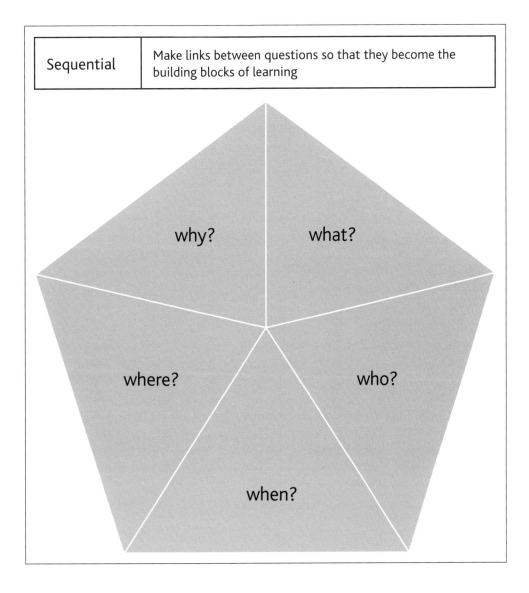

Higher order questions

Here is an example of the way in which learning outcomes, tasks and questions can be constructed to deliberately foster higher order thinking. Using any specific thinking framework as a 'question-designer' to create learning challenges is a way to ensure that high challenge is built into the learning opportunities on offer. It also works as the basis of a script for the conversations you will have with learners during the course of a lesson and the criteria for what you want to see, hear and sense as their thinking develops.

This question designer is particularly helpful in identifying what exactly you are asking students to *do* and how they need to be *thinking* (which also ties into what they need to be *like*). Not only is the level of challenge integral to the learning design but the assessment criteria is crystal clear, so you can communicate exactly what it is you are looking for when they are thinking 'well'. This means that learners can be actively involved in setting their own targets, assessing what they have achieved and what their next steps need to be. It also gives you a good idea of what it is you are looking for when assessing thinking, which, after all, can only be 'seen' when it is articulated either in what learners say or what they write. This one is structured around our old friend, the revised Bloom's taxonomy, which I've used throughout this book for consistency, but any thinking framework (de Bono's Thinking Hats or Biggs and Collis' SOLO Taxonomy[42] for example) can used to inform the specific activities we should be looking for when learners are thinking in a particular way.

---

42 Biggs and Collis http://www.johnbiggs.com/au/solo_taxonomy.html/

TAXONOMY	PROCESS VERBS	STUDENT
Create	compile, generate, design, produce, activate, devise, construct	reformulates, invents, presents
Evaluate	judge, rate, assess, weigh up, measure, defend, probe, argue, discuss, criticise, prioritise	makes decisions, disputes, clarifies
Analyse	distinguish, critique, compare, scrutinise, dissect, deconstruct, contrast, discern	discusses, debates, uncovers
Apply	experiment, deploy, connect, teach, adapt, practise, sketch, play out, rehearse	solves problems, clarifies processes
Understand	interpret, give examples, paraphrase, account for, explain, review, outline, retell, review	demonstrates, labels, summarises
Remember	define, name, record, list, organise, recite, distinguish, review, quote, reproduce	responds, absorbs, recalls

Targeted questions

Questions can be used to shape the culture of learning. This is an opportunity to mix things up and ensure that it really is the questions that are stimulating learning.

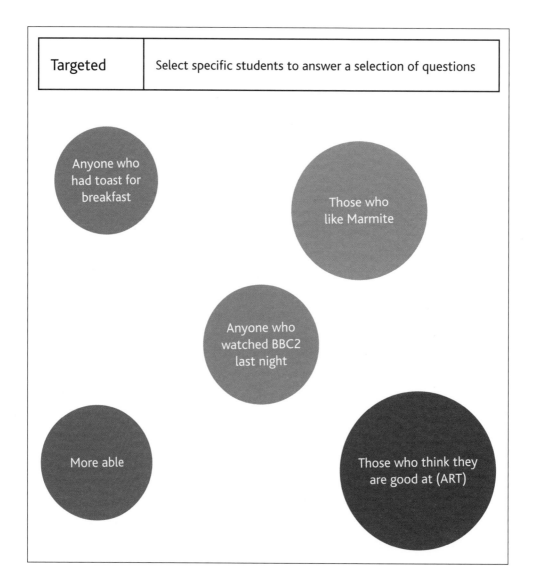

Choice

The way in which questions can be answered can also add variety to thinking. It can have the added benefit of enhancing collaborative learning or be used deliberately to promote creative thinking.

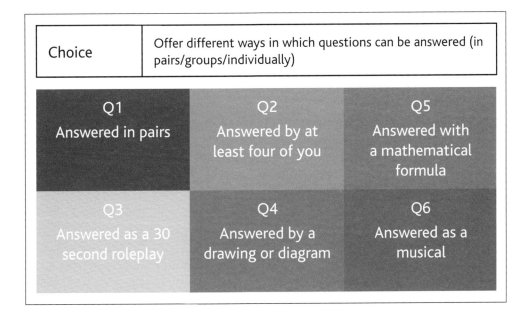

Choice	Offer different ways in which questions can be answered (in pairs/groups/individually)

Q1 Answered in pairs	Q2 Answered by at least four of you	Q5 Answered with a mathematical formula
Q3 Answered as a 30 second roleplay	Q4 Answered by a drawing or diagram	Q6 Answered as a musical

Authentically open questions

Open questions are critical to generating the richest possible responses. They are the highest order questions because they allow the student to lay the intricate facets of their thinking before you and their peers. Open questions invite the student to present a thinking narrative with deep explanations and often uniquely personal insights. This type of rich response inspires us all and can carry us through the rest of the day, so it's well worth trying to encourage it as often as possible.

If we interpret 'most able' or 'gifted and talented' simply as our most successful learners, then it is important to take into account what it is that these learners have been successful at doing. It is certainly true that they are very good at playing the well-known game of 'Guess what's in teacher's head?'. As such, when we ask a question, however well camouflaged as a genuinely unknown question, these learners have highly sensitive radars that enable them to hone in on and quickly reveal the *right* answer. All of this falls in line with the standard rules of learning engagement with which the 'quicker' learners are familiar: we ask, learner responds, we affirm. Although the question may be higher order, if there is still a built-in right or wrong answer, however well disguised, these learners are most likely to reveal it, and quickly. Which, in turn means that precious thinking gap we're trying to grow for everybody in the group gets closed.

An authentically open question is one to which there really is no right or wrong answer. It is posed to develop the disposition of *thoughtfulness* in and of itself. These types of question are an accelerant for enquiring minds. The openness frees them from trying to get the *right* answer and gives them permission to suggest what they think might be a *good* answer. They can argue their point of view, defend their stance and be judged on the quality of their thinking, not the accuracy of their response.

For others, and often those who are considered the most able, these questions need to be used, but used with care. You may ask genuinely unknown questions, and witness some of your class rapidly morphing into a group of highly anxious and under-confident individuals. They might avoid eye contact with you, start fidgeting and become reluctant to get involved. This might also happen if you *suddenly* present them with an unfamiliar start to the lesson like a creative thinking stimulus, an unusual picture or piece of music, a divergent thinking task or a simple 'What if?' challenge' especially if they are not used to being asked to think in such a 'free' way. By saying that there are no right or wrong answers, you are changing the rules of learning engagement. It is these rules that some of the most successful learners rely on. They make them feel safe. This is where the 'Why we are learning *like* this' explanation really comes to the fore and it is this that helps to guard against the tumble-weed effect described above.

Such an activity is a useful start-point for hypothesising, speculating and imagining. If you then overlay a topic, you can channel thinking down a particular pathway, encouraging them to apply their higher order thinking skills to the subject at hand. Mapped against any assessment criteria, they will quickly see the relevance of this way of learning. After time, however, I would hope that their understanding of such relevance will come not from examination assessment guidelines, but from seeing how thinking in this way is vital for them to prosper in the world at large; to *be* great thinkers.

Problems worth solving

Dan Meyer, a maths teacher from the United States, is on a mission to overhaul the way in which questions and problems are constructed in mathematics text-books in his fantastic blog.[43] His argument is that by presenting students with as much information as possible, many maths questions have the effect of closing down thinking rather than opening up an enquiring mind. He argues that in many instances, all students really need to do is rearrange the important pieces of infor-mation, so that they replicate the given formula and, hey presto, the solution can be found.

In his presentations and talks (readily available on the internet and via his blog), he uses this Einstein quote to drive home his point, 'The formulation of a problem is often more essential than its solution, which may be merely a matter of math-ematical or experiential skill'. Informed by Meyer's ideas in his TEDx Talk, 'Math class needs a makeover'[44], below is a formula for how students can start to construct their own problems. The nice thing is that it can be used in other subjects just as effectively.

---

43 See http://blog.mrmeyer.com.
44 Available at http://www.ted.com/talks/don.meyer_math_curriculum_makeover.html

1 **Present a simple and very brief stimulus** (e.g. picture, scenario, question, problem). You can do this or you can ask students to bring in their own.

2 **Ask questions like**: 'What do we already know about this? What questions does this prompt for us today? Where have we seen this or something like this before? What other subjects does this connect with? What does this remind us of?' and so on to assess prior knowledge and generate responses to the stimulus.

3 **Identify gaps in prior knowledge and understanding**, linked back to the original stimulus: 'What do we need to know about this if we are going to deepen our understanding/develop a thoughtful response/solve it?'

4 **Identify component pieces** of information that we already have or will need to have.

5 **Construct the problem.**

6 **Solve the problem.**

7 **Test the quality of the problem** according to agreed criteria of what makes a problem worth solving.

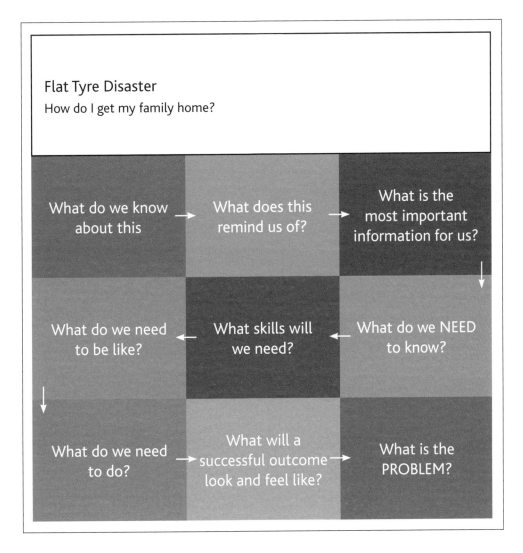

Flat Tyre Disaster
How do I get my family home?

What do we know about this	What does this remind us of?	What is the most important information for us?
What do we need to be like?	What skills will we need?	What do we NEED to know?
What do we need to do?	What will a successful outcome look and feel like?	What is the PROBLEM?

In addition to student-led problem construction, it is worthwhile trying to pose problems and scenarios that are real or at least highly likely to happen. This doesn't refer simply to placing problems in a real-world context and fabricating the information so it suits the purpose of what's next on the syllabus.

What are the characteristics of a problem *worth* solving?

Not all information available at the start

It matters to me

It takes time

It has *real* implications

It involves deep thought

It will need several people to solve it

Engaging with it will lead to personal development

It requires new knowledge

It affects/can involve many people

It demands concentration

It is complex and draws on a range of subject expertise

Solving it will result in measureable benefits

It is compelling

It will help develop new skills

It will lead to further discoveries

The crux is to make sure that the questions we pose are not only *related* to real-world events but can actually be *applied* to a real-world context. Cross-curricular projects are great for developing a sense of relevance, and leave us asking the learners to consider, 'When might you use this approach/way of thinking in school or beyond?' In this way, we can prevent learners from challenging with the age-old accusation, 'But when am I *ever* going to use this?'

The great thing is that the world is peppered with problems that need solving by economists, ethicists, philosophers, engineers, law-makers and so on. So by identifying the maths, science, geography or RE in current affairs or great historical events, we can apply subject-specific skills to create genuine context. In simple terms, this is all about remembering that common sense and subject-specific understanding can go happily hand in hand. When they are combined, students are far more ready to engage in the questions we ask and the problems we pose.

Purposeful Questioning

Quality questioning taps into what education, according to Germaine Greer, is really all about, 'The drawing out of what's inside'.[45] (In fact, this quote reflects the underpinning philosophy of Full On Learning). The overall purpose of questioning is to use questions to elicit ideas and thoughts from students for a specific purpose. This allows everybody involved to check out the accuracy and coherence of their thinking. This method can be used as a script by teachers and learners to establish quality learning conversations in our lessons.

---

45 Quote from *We Are The People We've Been Waiting For.* Available from http://wearethepeoplemovie.com

PURPOSE	EXAMPLE QUESTION STEMS
To help students build confidence and clarify their thinking	What exactly does that mean?
	Can you give me an example?
	Is that like ...?
	Why is that true?
	How did you reach that conclusion?
	Does that make sense?
	Why does that happen?
	What other methods would work here?
	Where will you get that information?
	Who can you check your answer/ideas with?
	Who can you demonstrate/explain to somebody else how you did that?
	How would you re-phrase this for a younger/less experienced student?
To test assumptions and promote problem-solving	Can you explain how you came to that view?
	What would happen if ...?
	What do you need to find out?
	What information do you already have?
	What strategies are you going to use?
	How will you attempt to find out?
	What/who might be able to help you?
	What do you think the answer will be?

To check out the reasoning behind statements and arguments

Would that work in all situations?

How might that apply to ...?

In what ways can you explain if that is true for all cases?

What would be an opposing argument?

How did you come to that decision?

How do you know that?

Are there any counter-examples?

How would you prove that?

What assumptions might you be making?

How would you explain to another group why your answer works?

How would you convince others that this is correct/the best way of doing it?

And why do you think that?

How would you rate this approach?

And ...?

Why ... why ... why?

To understand the stance or viewpoint taken and encourage empathy

Why is this better than ...?

What would an alternative view of this be?

How would you feel if ...?

How would (x) respond to this?

How do you think (x) thinks/feels/would respond to this?

What advice would you give to (x) about this?

How would that affect you?

How would somebody else (older/younger/different background) feel about this?

How does that (choice of vocabulary) affect the reader/audience/other group members?

What are the advantages/disadvantages of that happening to you/someone else?

PURPOSE	EXAMPLE QUESTION STEMS
To assess the implications of an argument or viewpoint and help secure understanding	How would that work with what we already know about this? How would this apply to …? What do you think about what (x) said? Do you agree? Why/why not? Does anyone have the same answer as you? Are there different ways to explain or show how to get to this answer? What different answers do you find most interesting? Do you understand what (x) is saying? How can you convince others that your answer makes sense? What effect is created by this? What makes this a good product/outcome? What are the key characteristics of this style/problem/question …? How are the key ingredients/components used in this example?
To get 'un-stuck' and develop resilience	How would you describe the problem in your own words? What do you know that is *not* stated in the problem? What do you *already* know and understand? What facts do you have? What information is/is not reliable here? How have you tackled similar problems in the past? What could you change/reduce/adapt to make this more manageable? How could you chunk the problem into two or three important parts? Would it help to create a diagram/picture/map/flow-chart etc. of your learning? How about having a guess and then attempt it? Have you compared your work with anybody else? What other methods have you/your group tried?

To play around with the question itself and encourage speculation

What is your understanding of the original idea/question?
Can you define what this means to you?
What would happen if ...? What if not ...?
If you did (x), what do you think would happen and why?
What could you do to change the outcome?
What do you think the intention of (x) is?
What would happen if you altered (*number*) things in the process/product?
Do you see any problems in what you have been shown?
What is likely to go wrong if you did (x)?
Are there any patterns that you can see/explain in this?
In what ways can you predict what happens next?
What do you think the final part of this will be?
What decision do you think (x) should make?

To make connections

How does this relate to?
Why do you think it is like this?
What else have we learnt today that is similar to this?
What ideas have we already had about this problem?
What is this similar to?
Are there any other ways to solve this?
What do you need to know to be able to complete the next step?
What does this relate to in the wider world/other subjects/previous topics?
What's the next step in the process?
What came before this process?

PURPOSE	EXAMPLE QUESTION STEMS
To support reflective and evaluative thinking (refer to success criteria of the lesson or activity to give these questions context)	How did you get your answer?
	Does this seem to make sense as a conclusion?
	What if you had started with (a) rather than (b)?
	How do you feel about how you did this?
	How would you rate your confidence/ability/knowledge/understanding etc. with this now?
	What did you know *before* you started this that helped you today?
	What choices did you and your group make to get to this point?
	Do you think you were successful in all aspects of the task?
	What did you need to *be like* to be able to complete this task?
	Were you successful – how do you know?
	How has your planning/research helped you come to this conclusion/with this idea?
	How can you make this even better?
	Why has this worked so well?
	What new information have you come across today?
	What new skills have you learnt today?
	What do you need to do better next time?
	What new technical information/words/methods have you used today that you hadn't used before?
	When were the key moments of learning from the lesson?
	What are the strengths of this?
	What would make this better?
	What were your BIG learning moments?

Philosophical enquiry

A very specific way to develop quality questioning is via Philosophy for Children.[46] P4C first came to mass attention following a documentary aired on the BBC in 1990 entitled Socrates for Six Year Olds. It highlighted the work of Dr Matthew Lipman and the development of communities of enquiry in classrooms. The aim is to encourage the type of deep thinking and reflection that characterised the cooperative debates and discussions of Ancient Greece. The children ask questions, select their line of enquiry and operate according to collaborative rules within their community of enquiry. The teacher acts as a facilitator of discussion, the most skilful of whom will barely utter a word throughout an entire discussion. The process is designed to deliberately encourage higher order thinking, reasoning and discussion and can be used with all ages and groups. The community of enquiry is guided by the four C's of good thinking:

 Critical – of ideas, not people. Taking a critical approach to the information, arguments and ideas that are presented.

Creative – in response to a stimulus (e.g. story, picture, film, piece of music). Connecting the power of imagination to the ability to formulate quality questions.

Collaborative – beyond just cooperation. A question is asked and the responses build, one after the other. When one student shares their thinking, the next student responds directly to that thought or argument, creating a collaborative web of ideas.

Caring – enquiry takes place in a climate of mutual trust and respect. There are agreed ground rules and a structured approach to ensuring that the enquiry is genuinely inclusive.

At the heart of any question-focused approach is the assertion that we learn best by *talking* things through. If we are able to articulate our thinking, we can hear it out loud, make sense of it and allow it to be challenged. The philosopher Antony

---

46 See the Society for Advancing Philosophical Enquiry and Reflection in Education (SAPERE) http://sapere.org.uk/

Flew argued that for any statement to be regarded as true, we must be able to say what evidence could be counted against it. In other words, unless our beliefs or assertions are allowed to be challenged, they lack value and meaning. From a Full On Learning point of view, unless we get the opportunity to share our thoughts, they are in danger of remaining unformed and lacking reason. If, on the other hand, we are required to share our thinking, not only do we have to articulate and therefore really understand our own thought processes, but we get to have our thoughts scrutinised by others. In doing so, we can practise our ability to reason and develop resilience in defending or persuading others of our thinking.

Action research

How can I use thinking frameworks (like Bloom's, de Bono, SOLO) to design question-focused learning opportunities?

How can I encourage learners to generate quality questions?

How can I support learners in understanding what a quality question looks, sounds and feels like?

How can I use questioning to promote creative thinking and intellectual risk-taking?

How can I use the language of 'thinking' to promote higher levels of engagement in learning discussions?

What questioning strategies can I use to 'hand over' learning? What do other teachers use in their learning stage/subject?

How can I develop my questioning so that it is specific and purposeful?

What question stems will 'drive' the learning?

What is the impact of using BIG and essential questions to 'anchor' learning and make it relevant?

 How do learners know that my questions are genuinely open?

How can I use a questioning/coaching approach to test out learners' inaccuracies and misconceptions?

 How can I use questioning to improve the quality of learning conversations during group work?

 How could giving learners a 'script' of questions improve the quality of self- and peer-assessment?

 How can I ensure that I use questioning consistently in each phase of a lesson?

EFFORT AUTONOMY
ENGAGEMENT REL

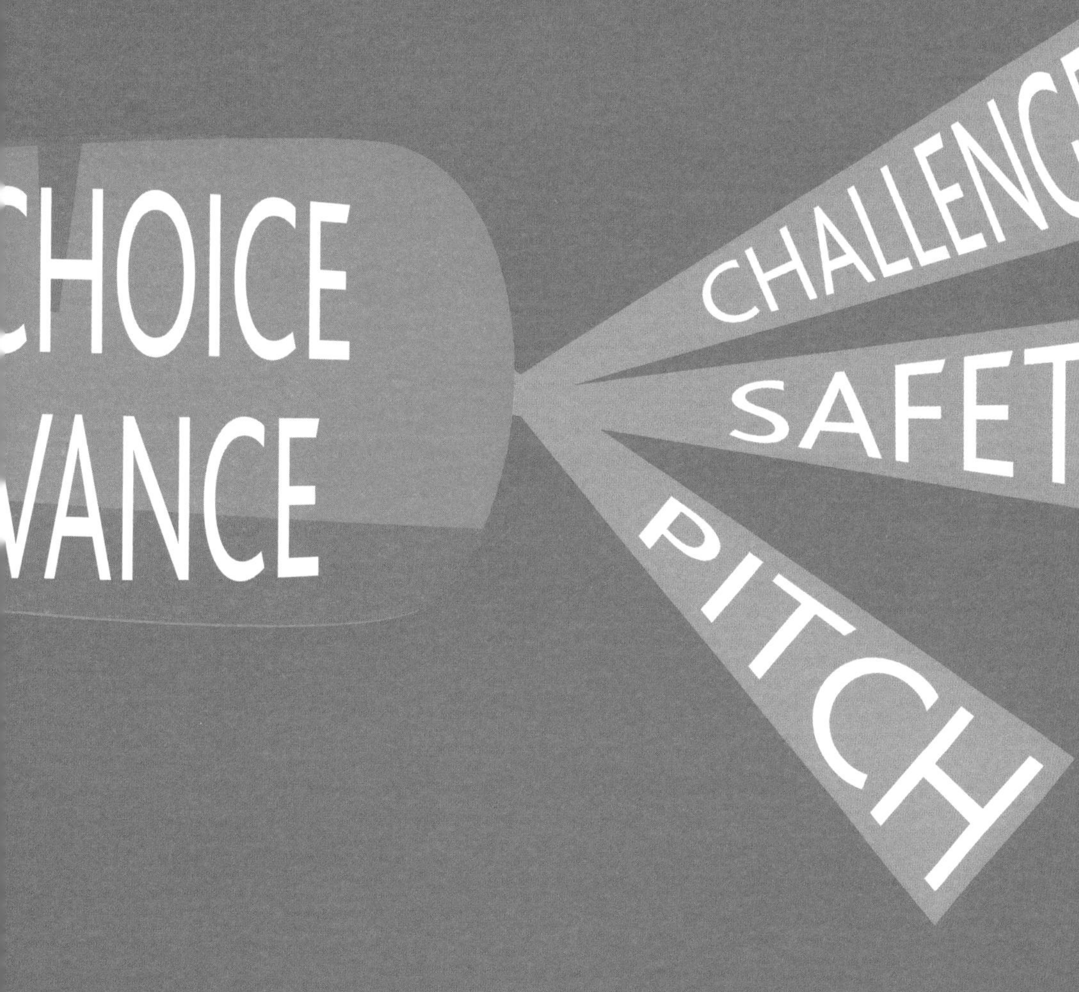

CHOICE
VANCE
CHALLENGE
SAFETY
PITCH

Choose to commit their time and effort to tasks they enjoy, find interesting and challenging because it matters to them

Designs learning challenges that are relevant to now and the future and have a clear purpose

Focus: rich challenges

Grow their knowledge and understanding when they listen to different views and perspectives that challenge their own thinking

Offers frequent opportunities for public presentations of understandings and peer-review. Engagement in discussions, debate and with 'experts' in the field

Focus: external expert panels

MOTIVATION

Selling dreams through learning

Carmine Gallo tracked the late Steve Jobs, former CEO of Apple, for over a decade to identify what it was that Jobs did and how he thought and innovated to make Apple Inc. the extraordinary success story that it is today.[47] Think about it: you can buy a standard laptop for a lot less than a MacBook. Furthermore, the Apple operating system is distinctly different from Windows, yet people are prepared (motivated) to switch and adapt to a new way of working. In fact, like any great brand, it has been suggested that when you buy an Apple computer, you 'buy into' Apple. As Seth Godin points out in his 'Standing Out' TED Talk, their success can be measured in their audience numbers who loyally tune into Steve Jobs's two-hour keynote addresses (which Godin refers to as two-hour advertisements) every six months that reveal the latest updates, products and innovations.[48] If we pose the question, 'If Apple designed learning, what would it be like?' we are already starting to get a good idea. Here is just one example of how one teacher responded (published on the Apple website following the release of iBooks 2 and iAuthor):

'... I am very excited ... I am forever asking students to put their iPads and phones away, and now I can provide them with fully interactive course information. Superb! This is [a] huge step forward for teachers, one that will allow us and students to fully embrace 21st Century Learning.'

---

47 Gallo, C., *The Innovation Secrets of Steve Jobs: Insanely Different Principles for Breakthrough Success* (Columbus, OH: McGraw-Hill, 2010).

48 Godin, S., Seth Godin on Standing Out (February 2003). Available at http://www.ted.com/talks/seth.godon_on_sliced_bread.html

Apple is *just one* example of the massive growth in the technology industry of the development of education-specific innovation for education. These companies have seen new ways to create powerful motivators for learning.

The thing that Steve Jobs did and Apple does, according to Gallo, is to 'sell dreams not products'. If you go into any Apple store, you won't find cashiers; only concierges and consultants. Why? Well, he says that it's because Apple's goal is to help you achieve your dreams, not to sell you *something*. The selling part is (almost) incidental to your dream. Apple's re-launch was marked with their legendary 'Think Different' campaign and since then, their message is simple: they want to make your life better, more functional, more aesthetically pleasing and more 'cool'. Almost as an afterthought, they say, 'Oh, and we'll do it by designing you a computer/music player/software programme that does a load of "super" stuff.' They leave the 'what' to the end of their message. The important bit is the engagement with our emotional self. It is this that is such an integral part of what motivates us to learn.

When I began teaching, my tutor said that the first thing I needed to do was to learn every student's name. The reason for this was that our name is the most 'attractive' word to us. If you know a student's name, you'll grab their attention straight away, even through a melee of industrious activity. She was absolutely right. The exciting challenge is whether we can construct learning so that it grabs the individual learner's attention in the same way – as if designed just for *them*, to meet *their* aspirations and dreams. If we can make the learning make sense to them – and enable them to see how it will benefit them – then we will be much closer to connecting with their sense of personal development and understanding of life-long learning. If learners feel involved in the learning process, they are more likely to be motivated to engage in it, because it matters to them. Because it is *for* them.

Blank timetable exercise

One way to tap into learners' likes and dislikes is the 'Blank Timetable' exercise. Print off a blank timetable and ask learners to fill it with the subjects that they enjoy at the times of the day and in the quantities they would like to have lessons in these. The key is to focus on the positive aspects of what learners already experience. You can also put restrictions on what they can do, how often and when. For example, you can stipulate that there must be at least three lessons of one subject and two of another. Another way to use it is to ask students to create 'subjects' they would want to spend time on when they're in school or to invite them to blur the boxes and re-design the school day according to their rationale. And it is just this rationale that you will be able to unpick during the process of completing the timetable.

You can also use this activity as a prompt for interviewing learners about how they choose to spend their free time, or as the basis for a learner voice programme, or as part of a mentoring programme, when conversations can sometimes be difficult.

Obviously, it's important to make it clear that it is *just an exercise* for them to share their thinking, just in case they think they are *actually* going to be able to revolutionise the timetable to five periods of Wii and three sessions of football (unless, of course, this is what they *are* going to be able to do). If you're lucky, you should be able to elicit some fantastic insights into what excites and motivates them. You may even get some good ideas for new projects or curriculum connections that tap directly into what they *want* to do and *how* they want to learn. If they, or you, for that matter, could invent subjects that you would like to do and that you think would be relevant for the future, what would you invent and why? At the very least, you will have a fantastic conversation about learning, plus you make a personal connection with them and this, in itself, is a compelling learning technique.

When it works, the dialogue between adult and learner is often far more meaningful as it allows the learners to share more about their personal interests than they would feel able to in a more formal teacher–learner setting. It also does a good job of breaking traditional subjects out of their own confines and offers us the chance to see what they enjoy, are good at and would like to develop. A central aspect of motivation is that we all like to feel involved and this activity fosters a real sense of belonging. One bonus might be that the exercise gives rise to some interesting educational projects that have school-wide benefit.

Motivation in action or 'flow'

When we are in what creative practitioners refer to as 'flow', time really does become relative. You will know that there are certain tasks that make you physically ache with boredom and which seem to take an eternity to complete. For my mum, this was always ironing on a Sunday evening. Interestingly, however, my dad would quite happily lose himself in the delicate art of pressing his uniform trousers at the same time every weekend. For him, time blissfully melted away as he created perfect creases. If we hate what we are doing, ten minutes can feel like ten hours. The other thing that happens when we're genuinely engaged is that it is the time when we 'come alive'. I am usually a very shy and quiet person (I have recently picked up the nickname of 'mole' thanks to my predisposition to work behind the scenes and stay 'underground') but if you get me talking about learning, it's as if you hit a 'full-power' button and I transform from quiet Mole to irrepressible Tigger. This is because I am very fortunate to have found what I love; the me-shaped space in the universe. And for teachers, once we find *our* own space, it becomes a personal mission to help others find theirs. And that's what we all want to do for our learners.

It is worth noting that what we choose to do in our free time, perhaps as a hobby when we are growing up, is often one of the best indicators of what we will end up doing in later life. In a world where many people are now able to create jobs to fit their passions, it's not a bad idea to foster those early enthusiasms and provide learning opportunities that develop the self-confidence and self-belief that will enable our learners to find and inhabit their 'me-shaped space'. Checking in with learners to see what really interests them so we can use our skill to help them make connections with their learning is a really powerful way to enhance motivation.

Involving learners in rewards

Finding out what it is that makes students put in the hard graft to do well in exams is extremely worthwhile. If you also video the conversations, you end up with a very powerful resource to share with other learners and staff, not to mention the next cohort of wavering GCSE students and their parents, carers and teachers. The message that is likely to come through is simply, 'We wanted the best grades possible'. The reward they seek is often highly personal and intrinsic. Like acquiring extra powers in a video game, there is a great deal of intrinsic satisfaction from applying yourself to a challenge and then seeing a job well done. Especially when it comes with direct and instant feedback.

So in what ways can we make learning as engaging, memorable and unmissable as the next release of the most popular computer game? Building in instant feedback systems might be one way (sticky notes are great for this, see Chapter 7 on Feedback) but it is also worth consulting students in the design of any aspect of school systems. You could pose a challenge along the lines of, 'If schools operated a loyalty card scheme, what learning "rewards" would students want to collect?' or 'What constitutes a reward for you?'

Similarly, creating opportunities for learners to recognise clear and tangible incremental progression during a lesson or series of lessons maintains the link between prior, present and future learning and places it in the context of the bigger learning design questions of 'why', 'how' and 'what' that we met earlier. It could be argued that the 'reward' of learning is simply the goodie bag of levels, grades and qualifications regarded as the currency of learning today. But dig a little deeper and it is the sense of effort well applied that really seems to make most of us buzz because it lets us know that we can actually 'do it' and 'we get it'.

Intrinsic motivation

According to science, sociology and psychology, humans like to feel that they have control over their lives. We like to be able to make real choices or at least be involved in the decision-making. That's one of the reasons why holidays and week-ends are so popular; it's (theoretically) the time when we get to do what we *choose* to do. Building choices into lessons can have the same effect.

Interestingly, for most of us, having independence over our own life doesn't equate to sitting around all day watching TV. We generally *prefer* to be productive. The reason for this is that we can experience a sense of purposeful achievement – why else do we take up new hobbies or leisure activities? The reward for doing so is not winning a huge record deal, opening our own exhibition or achieving monetary gain. In pursuing our hobbies and interests, we can fulfil our own sense of personal achievement and growth. We get to learn.

The Four Ts of Autonomy

We know that offering real choices to learners about what, how and when they learn is crucial to fostering autonomous learning. This leads to a desire for mastery, whether this is a specific skill or more concerned with deepening our understanding of a new concept. We want to get better at 'stuff' because the purpose of doing so is clear to us. Humans respond positively when they are able to take control of their learning. To do this, however, we must see purpose in what we are being asked to do and learn to develop the confidence, understanding and skills necessary to take appropriate decisions about our individual learning pathways.

Building autonomy into lessons can be a challenge. Going whole-scale with autonomy rarely works as an introduction, so consider splitting the components of learning into the Four 'T's used by companies such as Google.[49]

---

49 Daniel Pink mentions Google's use of time, task, team and technique in his 2009 TED Talk 'On the surprising science of motivation' http://www.youtube.com/watch?v=rrkrvAUbU9Y

1 **Task** – what we have to complete/learn/produce

2 **Team** – who we will work with (self, pairs, groups)

3 **Time** - when we need to complete each task or part of task

4 **Technique** – how we will complete it (materials, product and process)

The rule of thumb is to gradually build the number of choices available to the learners, so you need only select one or, at most, two of these 'T's for the learners to make decisions about. For example, you can ask the group to take responsibility for the Technique – how the task will be completed whilst you set the time limits, the focus of the task and the groups that they learn with.

You can them work with them to agree success criteria for each 'T' (including the one they have responsibility for) and these criteria will inform your reflection and progress-checking questions as the lesson moves on.

Fostering effort-focused-awareness

Nobody can make anybody genuinely learn anything if they don't want to. We learn because something hooks us in. We continue to learn because we find the challenge of development exciting and rewarding. Remember Carol Dweck, and her 'fixed' and 'growth' mindsets.[50] Growth mindsets are characterised by an insatiable desire to develop, improve and achieve. She asserts that we can teach a growth mindset so that engagement, intrinsic motivation and productivity will increase.

---

50 Dweck, C. S., *Mindset: The New Psychology of Success* (New York: Random House, 2006).

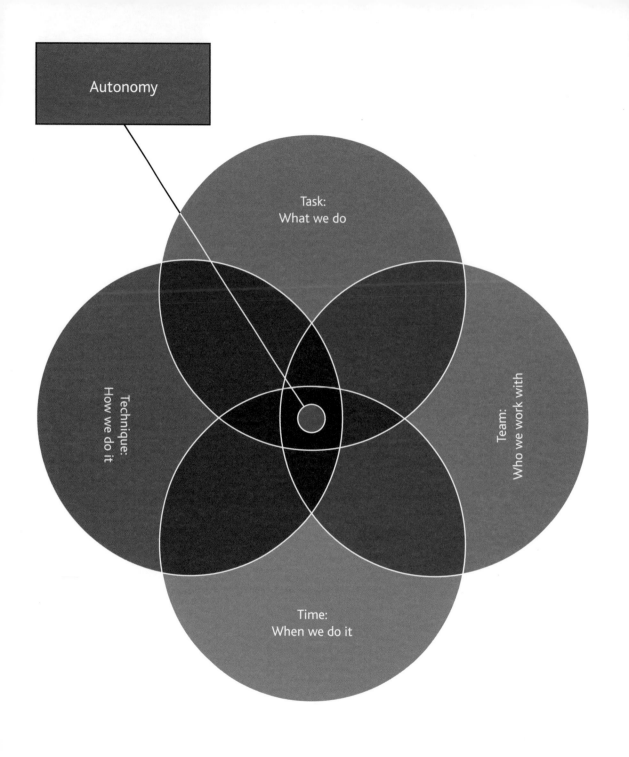

> If *you* were given a 'free time' token to work on anything you choose for 20% of your time every week, what would you work on?

> If you gave your students a 'free time' token to work on anything they choose for 20% of their time every week, what *could* they *create?*

Source: Daniel Pink TED[51]

The growth mindset develops when the conditions for learning are safe, the rationale for the learning challenge is communicated using the 'why', 'how' and 'what' framework and the tasks we ask learners to do are realistic and purposeful. The language of learning used in the classroom should promote and value the learning process, and the thinking that underpins it, as being *as* important or even more important than the achievement of a final product.

Here is one approach that unapologetically values process over product:

 The teacher explains that over the next four lessons, the focus will be on *how* well you learn, rather than *what* you produce.

Each learner is required to keep a journal of their thoughts, reflections and observations. These can be writings, photographs, cuttings, relevant links and clips – it is entirely up to the individual learners.

Milestones or 'check-in' points are agreed for the duration of the project to ensure everybody is making good progress.

 At the end of the fourth lesson, with their final work completed, the teacher takes the finished pieces of work and puts them to one side.

 The learners then have to summarise the thoughts, reflections and progress that they have recorded in their journals.

51 www.ted.com/talks/dan_pink_on_motivation.html

6 The final session of reflection *only* discusses the *process* they have been through at this point, not the final product (this is made easier as their work is out of sight).

Creating a definite break between process and product means that we can give explicit value to each learner's efforts, learning capacities and dispositions. Once they know that the focus will be on *process*, learners may well become more adventurous, more accepting of things not working out and find that their efforts leave space for surprises. The result is that they become motivated to get involved in their own learning process. The quality of reflection is also a definite winner in this scenario. Moving the final products out of sight and asking learners to present their documents of learning first focuses conversations on what is important at that moment. It is almost as if the visible presence of a final product is a distraction that anchors the conversation to the end point, making it difficult to reflect on the progression that has been made. If the final product is sitting in full view, possibly with a grade or level attached to it, it is *really* difficult to ask learners to reflect on the process of learning because it feels like this is not what is being measured and valued. Even if they have invested enormous effort in completing the task, if they perceive their end-product to be inferior to that of their peers, it will only be a very self-confident person who says, 'I may well have one of the worst pieces of work in the group, but I tried really hard.'

In focusing on the learning process in splendid isolation, conversations can be about, 'How do you feel now in comparison with how you felt at the start of the lesson? What did you do to overcome difficulties? What would you do differently next time? What were you most pleased with about how you approached the task?' After learners (and teachers) have become accustomed to this way of working, you can mix and match the process/product lessons and start to develop a more equal weighting between learning process and final product. Once learning has been drawn out from the process conversation, a celebration of the product can then happen, seeing it as a component part of the whole learning experience. All of this helps to nurture a 'can-do' environment, which in turn motivates us to be resilient and keep trying.

Worthwhile learning

As we have already seen, one way in which we can design worthwhile learning experiences is to tap into the world of the learner to create the hook. We can also co-construct learning using principles borrowed from business such as '20 per cent time' in the curriculum. This concept is drawn from companies like Google, Disney and Pixar who ask employees to fill 20 per cent of their work-time with a project or activity of *their own choosing*. This might be a project entirely unrelated to their day-to-day role or working with a team of people with whom they would not ordinarily be involved. Some companies have taken this approach even further and structure the whole working week around the premise that individuals can work on their own projects, so long as they deliver to the deadline they agree with their line manager.

The 20 per cent time approach could be tried (using the Four Ts approach) in an individual lesson, a project that covers several lessons, a day or even a week.

Involving learners in a discussion around what their learning should look, sound and feel like is a powerful way to tap into motivation, as does giving degrees of choice, because it makes it personal to them. Asking learners to identify the level of chal-lenge they are prepared to experience during the lesson and then asking them to assess what they actually encountered by the end of the lesson can nurture their 'can-do' thinking. Discussing what learners need to 'be like' in addition to what they need to know, understand and be able to do can similarly foster a growth mindset. All, or some of these ideas can be used to shape the success criteria of the task and reiterate the 'Where you are, where you need to be and how you're going to get there?' learning conversation.

Tapping into the elusive key that unlocks the motivation of learners requires a whole range of strategies. That's where our *own* motivation comes in. Because we know exactly what it looks, sounds and feels like for us and for our learners when we *do* find that key.

Action Research

How can I stimulate intrinsic motivation for learning and what does motivated learning look, sound and feel like?

How do I develop greater learning awareness in me/learners/colleagues?

How can I use creative approaches to learning to stimulate engagement?

How can I design opportunities for learners to take control and make decisions about their own learning?

How can learners make genuine choices about their learning pathways when we've got a curriculum to get through?

How can I support learners to construct their own learning and develop a 'can-do' approach?

How can I find out if my learners have a 'growth' or 'fixed' mindset?

What is the language of a 'growth' or 'fixed' mindset so I can identify it in lessons?

How can I communicate the point of what we are doing to learners in a variety of different ways?

LEARNERS WHO ...	TEACHING THAT ...
Enjoy finding unconventional methods and processes to gain new knowledge and skills	Learning processes are acknowledged alongside learning outcomes
	Provides regular opportunities for decision-making and problem-solving.
	Focus: feedback explicitly focuses on the process of learning
Manage risk well when faced with challenging situations and tasks. They are prepared to 'go out on a limb'. They respond positively to setbacks from which they are eager to learn. They can plan their next steps and are confident to take them	Integrates choice into selected aspects of learning.
	Encourages learners to take responsibility for the learning opportunities they encounter.
	Focus: offer limited choices (time or activity or outcome or group)

LEARNING ENTREPRENEURS

Here's to the crazy ones. The rebels. The troublemakers. The ones who see things differently. While some may see them as the crazy ones, we see genius. Because the people who are crazy enough to think they can change the world, are the ones who do.[52]

The term *Learning Entrepreneur* exists in a number of other works where the characteristics of entrepreneurialism are explored and connected with learners. One use of the term is found in Douglas Thomas and John Seely Brown's book, *A New Culture of Learning*.[53] Here, however, the term 'Learning Entrepreneur' refers to those specific learning **dispositions** that we need to nurture and develop in an effective learner. The characteristics of somebody who is considered entrepreneurial in the business world can easily be matched against many generic lists of characteristics we might come up with when answering, 'What do we want our students to be able to do and to be like?'

52 Giles, N. and Hayman, M., *Disruptive Influence: The Entrepreneur Report from Virgin Media Pioneers* (2010). Available at http://www.virginmediapioneers.com/files/2010/09/Disruptive-Influence-The-Entrepreneur-Report.pdf.

53 Douglas, T. and Seely Brown, J., *A New Culture of Learning: Cultivating the Imagination for a World of Constant Change* (CreateSpace, 2011).

The change mantra

In any environment where there is significant change - and the world of education experiences more than its fair share - there will always be opportunities to innovate and 'think different'. And that's where our expert pedagogues can come in. We need to be ready to shape those opportunities for ourselves and claim them as the spaces where every learner can discover their capacities and thrive. Full On Learning can do just this. With a skilful and relentless focus on drawing out the individual capacities of every young person, the spaces that we identify can become the place where creativity and thoughtful personal development incubate. Which brings us to the concept of the learning entrepreneur.

Wealth in wisdom

Richard Cantillon (1680s–1734) was an Irish-French economist and is known as the originator of the term 'entrepreneur'. Since its original economic interpretation, the term has been used in a variety of contexts to describe innovation, creativity, ingenuity and the ability of an individual or group to exploit an opportunity in an unexpected way.

What is interesting about entrepreneurialism is that it is often perceived (like creativity, 'giftedness' and intelligence) as something that you either do or do not have. In addition, the success of any business entrepreneur is usually judged on their accumulated wealth and these achievements are often explained away to luck. Take this quote from Biz Stone, co-founder of Twitter, 'We got lucky – it doesn't mean we're geniuses.' This kind of statement really doesn't help our learners. It makes it seem like success is just one part of life's lottery, over which we have very little control, and trying to convince a disengaged student to aspire to achieving their target grade suddenly becomes a whole lot harder. On the whole, when you ask successful individuals themselves, however, you usually get a very different picture. In a recent piece of research carried out by Virgin Pioneers, ten successful entrepreneurs were interviewed about the factors and drivers for their success.[54] The

---

54 Giles and Hayman, *Disruptive Influence*, p. 14.

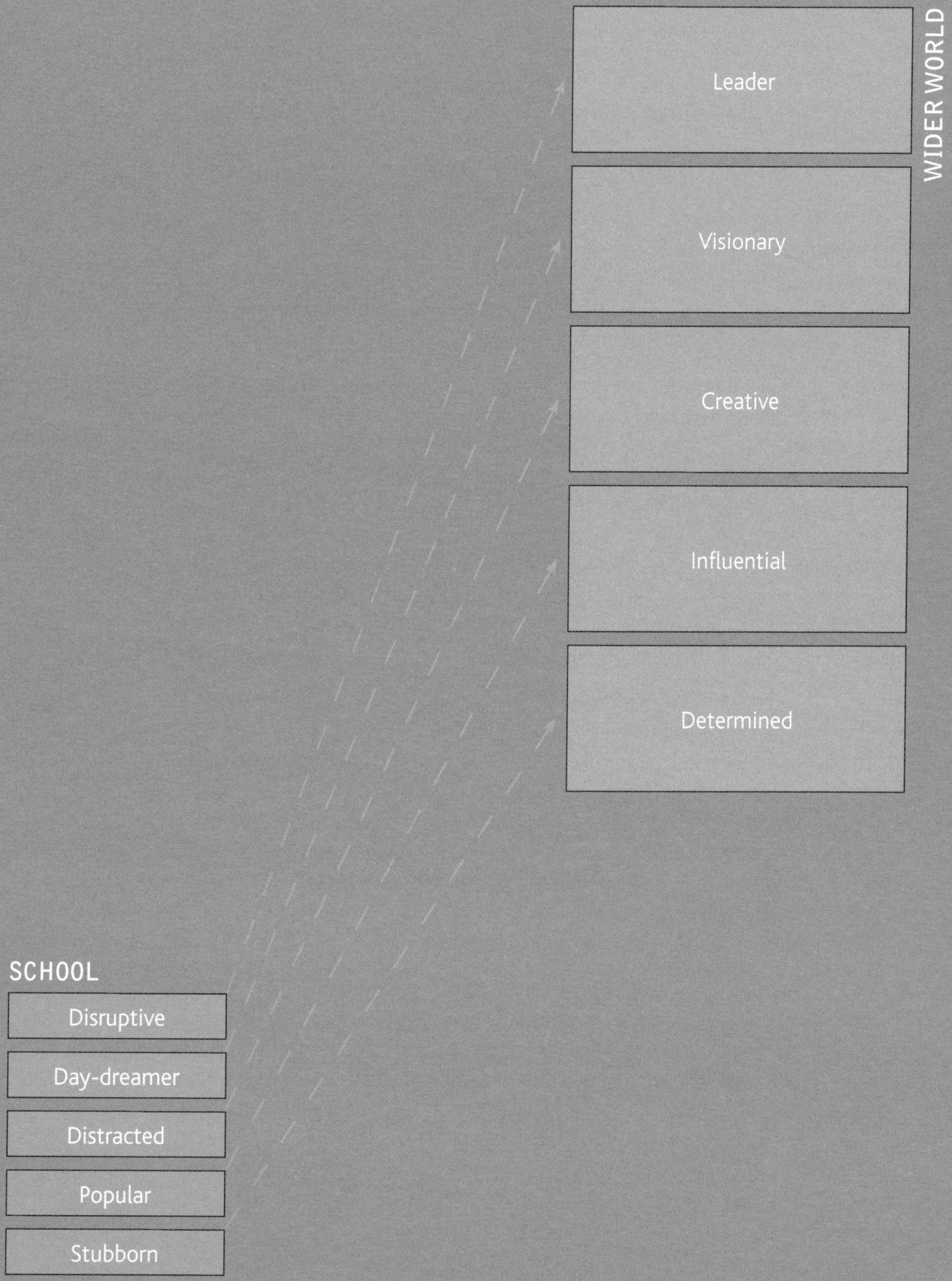

WIDER WORLD

Leader

Visionary

Creative

Influential

Determined

SCHOOL

Disruptive

Day-dreamer

Distracted

Popular

Stubborn

researchers observe that the behaviours deemed essential to becoming a successful entrepreneur often mean the individuals are regarded as 'disruptive influences' in younger life.[55]

When we assess learners' behaviour, we are often subconsciously considering how appropriate it is in context. If the behaviour doesn't adhere to acceptable conventions, we quite rightly see it as unacceptable and take steps to correct it. But it is always worth at least considering the learners' own interpretation of the 'contextual appropriateness' of their behaviour.

I learnt an invaluable lesson when once teaching an RS A-level group. The new batch of students were still delighting in their novel status as sixth-formers and I would get them discussing and debating early on in the course so that they had as much time as possible to practise their thinking out loud ahead of having to write their arguments in essay form. One student came to the course with the minimum number of points and special dispensation to enter the sixth form. His GCSE results reflected disappointing underachievement and he had a reputation as being a joker and distracter in class. In an introductory discussion about the 'ethical norms' of behaviour, conduct and laws, he remained passive and apparently disinterested. In an effort to get him to engage, I asked him what factors he felt were important in the development of a society.

'Clothes,' he answered, without looking up. The group looked confused and then started laughing. He smiled too. Still no eye contact. I did not smile. I assessed what had just happened and (too) quickly labelled his answer as deliberately disruptive. Not only that, but I supported my interpretation with an internal narrative that reassured me that he was not paying attention (he was doodling during the discussion) and not contributing (he failed to offer any interpretations of his own or give me eye contact). So, I reasoned, when I asked him a direct question he replied with the first and most obscure thing that came into his head (a) out of panic at being caught out and (b) intending to diffuse my attention by getting the group to laugh.

Before I took this opportunity to remind him of the expectations of engaging in A levels, I decided to call his bluff. 'Interesting idea,' I said, 'Please would you explain that a bit more?' His answer, however, was absolutely brilliant. It went something like this, 'Clothes are a fundamental aspect of any society. What we consider to be

---

55 Giles and Hayman, *Disruptive Influence*, p. 18.

decent or indecent usually starts with the way in which we dress, which reflects a whole heap of our personal values, our class, our economic and societal status. Clothes can also get you into a load of trouble. If you get dress code wrong in a country, you can end up deeply offending people or even contravening the law.'

I was *so* wrong. His answer betrayed a real flair to his thinking that would guide him through the course (in his own very unique way) on his journey to university. To this day, I use this incident to remind myself that not everybody's brain works in the same way (as mine) and nor can I trust my interpretation of their body language. Yet another reason to stand back, observe and then ask, not tell.

A creative, imaginative and entrepreneurial thinker will often find that what they say, do and think is frequently negatively labelled. It is seen as wrong or disruptive, contravening the social conventions of learning. All of which means that we miss a certain sort of brilliance.

Compare, on the one hand, a definition of entrepreneurial thinking ('disruption' in the Virgin Pioneers report) from Sir Richard Branson:

> Disruption is all about risk-taking, trusting your intuition and rejecting the way things are supposed to be[56]

with the definition of Creative Thinking from QCA's personal, learning and thinking skills (PLTS):

> Young people think creatively by generating and exploring ideas and making original connections. They try different ways to tackle a problem, working with others to find imaginative solutions and outcomes that are of value. Young people:

- generate ideas and explore possibilities
- ask questions to extend their thinking
- connect their own and other's ideas and experiences in inventive ways
- question their own and other's assumptions

56 Adapted from Giles and Hayman, *Disruptive Influence.*

◼ try out alternatives or new solutions and follow ideas through

◼ adapt ideas as circumstances change.[57]

The term 'learning entrepreneur' is concerned with wealth acquisition, but *not* about *monetary* wealth. The wealth of a learning entrepreneur is measured in terms of wisdom, curiosity and an infinite capacity to learn. It is not about status in terms of kudos and position but rather the self-confidence and assuredness that comes from successful creative learning achievements. It is not about influence in terms of power over people or circumstance but in terms of bringing about positive change for the individual and for society as a whole.[58] It is important, then, that if we are to develop expertise in learning entrepreneurialism, that we know what to look out for.

Organic learning

Full On Learning reflects more of an agricultural model of learning rather than an industrial one. The role of the teacher is akin to that of a skilful and attentive gardener who understands and can harness a range of ecological factors to design an appropriate learning environment. She can employ a personalised care routine or feedback system for each of her 'plants' that enables her to step back and watch them blossom or intervene as and when they are ready. The Full On Learning garden is designed to produce an exciting crop of learning entrepreneurs who will emerge from their environment with the necessary hardiness and tenacity to go out into the wider world and inspire and excite others. The criteria for success are that outcomes must be tangible and measurable according to the values of individual learners and the wider society. The following table matches up the qualities of entrepreneurialism from the Virgin Pioneers report with learning behaviours and dispositions we can develop in our classrooms.

---

57 http://curriculum.qcda.gov.uk/uploads/Personal%2C%20learning%20and%20thinking%20skills%20leaflet_tcm8-12831.pdf.

58 Adapted from Giles and Hayman, *Disruptive Influence*.

ENTREPRENEURIAL SKILLS AND DISPOSITIONS

Hire the right people. Listen to them

Set the standard: no one will care more about your business than you

Do your research. Understand your customer, your product and your market. Be prepared

Move on. Don't dwell in the past. Learn from your mistakes and move on. Actively seek feedback

Trust your instinct. Believe in yourself

Take risks. Take action

Develop expertise (yours and other's). Build a dynamic team. Bring in a blend of skills and experience

LEARNING ENTREPRENEURIAL SKILLS AND DISPOSITIONS

Build effective relationships with your peers/team

Care about what you are learning and developing and communicate this in what you do

Research carefully to construct your knowledge and deepen your understanding. Think through what you are doing and get into the habit of contingency planning by posing 'What if?' questions

Learn from feedback and use this to inform your next steps. Seek out people and resources that will help you progress

Be courageous. Articulate a clear rationale for the decisions you make. Be confident in your abilities

Take intellectual risks. Try new approaches. Have a go at things you don't feel confident about immediately. Confidence comes from experience, not the other way around

Be self-aware. Know your own skills and recognise the skills of your team. As a whole team, work to your strengths and find ways to develop other areas together

ENTREPRENEURIAL SKILLS AND DISPOSITIONS	LEARNING ENTREPRENEURIAL SKILLS AND DISPOSITIONS
Never give up. Be persistent. It's important to sometimes be wrong, otherwise you won't know what right looks like	Be resilient. You only learn when you are faced with situations that are new to you and to which you don't know the answer
Be passionate about what you do. Passion and persistence are critical	Commit to your own learning because it's all about you. If you don't care, no one will
Keep evolving. Have a relentless focus on innovation	Be wise about the world and be adaptable to its changing demands.
Tell the truth	Act with integrity at all times. Be honest
Have a vision. Let your imagination drive your thinking. Enjoy the journey and learn from this	Be aspirational and creative. Give yourself time to think divergently (with play and imagination) and convergently (with purpose and value). Value the process of learning
Be results oriented	Know what you want to achieve, have clear success criteria and know how you are going to achieve this. Ask for feedback to help you progress

Action research

How can I use learning objectives/outcomes to explicitly encourage qualities of innovation and creativity?

What does innovation look, sound and feel like in (subject/topic/school) for (a) me as a teacher and (b) learners?

How can I develop my feedback language to promote a growth mindset in all my learners?

In what ways do I communicate and promote a passion for learning through my lesson design?

How can I use group work to promote sharing of ideas and working in different ways?

What strategies can I develop to give learners regular opportunities to 'Think Different'?

What is a 'risk' for me in my own practice?

How often do I take 'risks' in my own practice and how can I model this for my learners?

How do I communicate high expectations in the written feedback I provide?

What impact does my oral feedback have on my learners' progress?

BEWARERE
OF THE BULL

OVER TO YOU

Beware of the bull

My mum spent an inordinate amount of time on her final assessment piece at art college. She describes it as 'one of the most beautiful and carefully designed pieces of illustration I have ever produced'. It is not for this reason, however, that she remembers it so well. On the completion of her masterpiece, she invited her best friend to see it before it was mounted for the end of year exhibition. In bold red capital letters the warning message shouted out for all to read (not least her examiners) but horror of horrors was the typo in the tagline, 'Bewarere of the Bull'. To this day, my mum remembers that even when her friend tentatively alerted her to the error, it took her a good two minutes before she could see the mistake for herself.

We all know that there are times that we are too close to what we are doing to spot problems that are obvious to others. We develop a default setting during our early days of classroom practice and the next thing we know we are repeating familiar strategies, reciting mantras of our own and are in danger of becoming a bit stale. There are times when we need a default setting to fall back on, a teacher's autopilot, like those days when we're coming down with the latest bug, or the heating just won't turn down. The trick is to be as critical of this mode of teaching as we are about the *new* things we experiment with. The problem of the expert, covered in Chapter 4, is closely linked to this.

There is a joy to discovering innovations in learning; not just taking new ideas and using them but extracting the principles that make them effective. These can then be used to shape new approaches, appropriate in new contexts. Working this way has a number of benefits:

 In understanding pedagogical principles underlying great ideas, the activities become valuable illustrations that can easily be added to and reinvented. This makes for sustainable learning design.

 We can employ our professional expertise and local intelligence to ensure that the principles can be successfully used to enhance learning in our own lessons and with our own students.

3   We take responsibility to think and create knowledge and understanding for ourselves, in the same way that we ask students to think and create knowledge and understanding for themselves.

4   We avoid the trap of being perceived as the 'expert teacher' which, let's face it, is a pretty massive burden. The collective expertise in any school or cluster of schools will far outweigh the individual expertise of one teacher or two teachers, however good they are.

So, adopt – then adapt – simple (but effective) ideas to make them last

Taken as it is, without any adaptation, the 'Would you rather … ?' activity works well as a creative thinking/talking starter. There's no real problem in using it in this way. But if you do so, be warned that it may have a very short shelf-life. This is one of the major disadvantages of the archetypal beginning-of-term INSET day when the whole staff are introduced to a collection of new activities. In about three weeks, the students will roll their eyes and moan as you innocently and enthusiastically introduce the second of your new repertoire of tools – only to be told by them that they've been doing that activity in every lesson since the beginning of term. If, on the other hand, we are inspired by INSET sessions to *adopt* and *adapt* our *own* activities, then the chances are we'll almost certainly improve upon the initial idea. A good idea is a good idea because it can be *adapted* to work in a variety of contexts. Whilst the underlying principles remain the same, the way in which it is used and the context in which it used is subject to change.

For example, the idea that underpins the apparently simple 'Would you rather?' example is that students are far more effective in comparative thinking if the choices they are given are restricted in some way. In addition, you can build in some form of incremental challenge by presenting comparative concepts that, with each iteration, become more and more closely related. After all, having to choose between two closely related options is what *makes* it a hard choice. If you ask the learners to adapt the activity to a subject-specific context, you can provide them with an opportunity to have some great learning debates.

In this example, the choice is between trying to survive in a Brazilian rain forest or a *favela*. In science, it might be between being haemoglobin or a platelet. In English, in might be between being Macbeth or Lady Macbeth. These activities employ similar open-ended philosophically based principles that you will find in activities such as Ian Gilbert's popular 'Thunks',[59] but with the added element of comparison to enable students to practise different thinking skills.

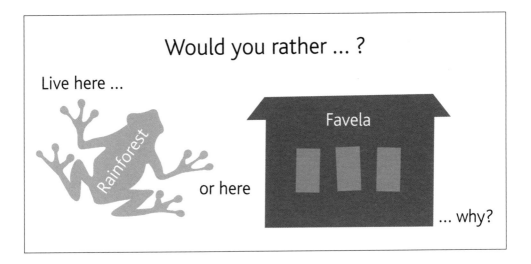

---

59 See http://www.independentthinking.co.uk/Cool+Stuff/Thunks/default.aspx.

Reflective professional development

One of the drivers for all teachers – and the thing that keeps us in the profession beyond the first few years – is that teaching is fundamentally a creative activity. We constantly seek out diverse, new ways to explain, coach and empower learners. Even when a particular unit of work performs really well, we will find ourselves tweaking and adapting it to make sure it really hits the mark every time we teach it. After all, if we are teaching to the strengths and needs of every learner, it doesn't make sense to teach the same topic in the same way every year and expect the same impact every time. When it comes to teaching, the job is never 'done'. Furthermore, if we are teaching to involve authentically every learner, then we need to constantly use *their* ideas, experiences and responses to inform *our* methodology and ensure relevance.

An integral component for creative practice is our ability to step back and reflect on what we are doing, which is what really effective professional development allows us to do. In this way, we can inform our next steps and be sure that we address issues along the way. It is vital, therefore, that we nourish our teaching creativity so that we are able to enrich the learning opportunities we offer and, just as importantly, enhance our own thinking.

Mirror, mirror on the classroom wall

If we were to hold a mirror to our own practice, what would we (a) want to see reflected in it and (b) actually see? If there is a difference between the two images, this is not a problem. That's what we would expect. For the learning geek in all of us, that's a learning appetite we can feed. But we don't know what to feed it until we've looked hard at what is already there. That's where our vital role as the reflective practitioner needs to come to the fore.

Working in a climate of reflective practice is a vital strand of great professional development, especially when it is fully integrated as a systemic, school-wide, cultural approach to teaching and learning. In the frenetic world of the school, time for

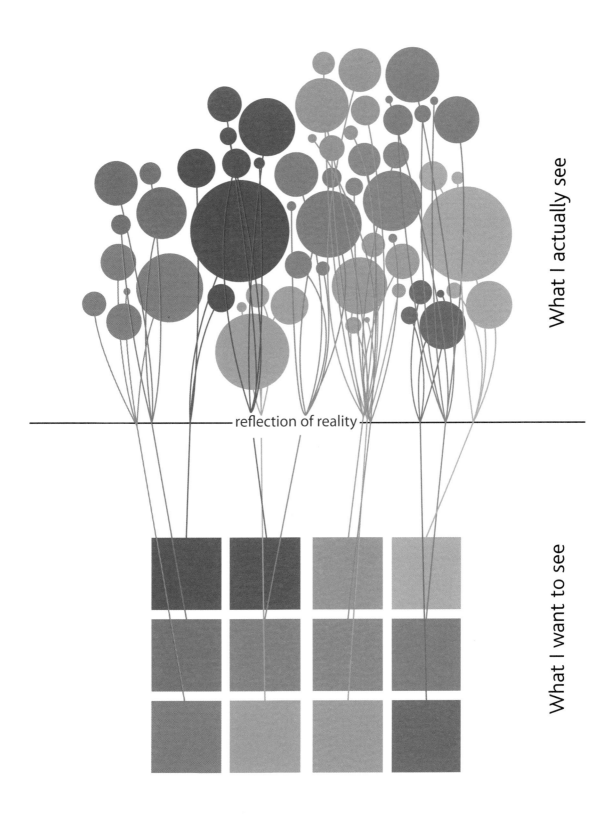

What I actually see

reflection of reality

What I want to see

quality self-reflection can feel so precious to the extent of it being perceived as an unrealistic luxury. But it is essential that we find the time to reflect and develop our practice as a *part* of our practice. Often, we miss great practice happening in our own schools, possibly just down the corridor from us ...

 1 Who could you invite to come and see what you are doing with a particular group and help you assess its effectiveness?

2 Who would you like to see doing 'their thing' with one of their groups?

3 What aspect of AfL/technology/group work/creative learning do you know, in your heart of hearts, you avoid?

 4 Is there anybody in your school who does the above regularly and seems to be comfortable with it?

 5 What aspect of your pedagogy could you offer to others for them to come and see it in action?

 6 How would you design opportunities to stand back and observe the impact of your teaching on the quality of learning during your own lessons?

7 What area of your subject teaching would you like to evaluate through some action research/student voice/learning walks/lesson observations?

 8 When might you find time in a week to take 10 minutes out and reflect on the way in which your learners are making progress/engaging with their own learning/developing group work skills as a result of your teaching practice?

Action research

Action research is a fantastic way to support professional learning and development. You begin with a commitment to start investigating a specific question and use a 'thinking framework' which can be as simple as 'plan-do-review' to identify your own learning outcomes, your mode of evidence collection and your systems to share your learning along the way. As with all the most powerful learning opportunities, it is the *process* that is the real change-maker, above any tangible action or change in pedagogy that results from the research.

There are many different enquiry frameworks available, but the key ingredients of effective action research are listed below. Some elements might be undertaken at different stages, so you may wish to jump around and visit different aspects at various stages.

1   **Build social capital**. Often teachers undertake action research as part of a group, therefore you need to invest time in getting to know each other. You may already know one another as colleagues but this is different. You are now learners. There will be times when you feel uncomfortable, vulnerable, under-confident or, quite simply, shattered. There is no substitute for building and maintaining high quality relationships. At the outset, progress in terms of getting on and doing will probably feel slow because you may feel you are not really doing anything. But rest assured you are. In addition, this is one area where you can deliberately practise the art of community building for your lessons. You can try out ice-breaker activities, creative thinking starters and other strategies helpful for entering into group work. Google 'team building activities' for businesses or creative design companies and see if there are any novel games or strategies you could adopt and adapt. Starting a meeting with, 'I found this on the internet, I've never tried it, so it may be dreadful, but I thought we could give it a go' sets a fun, creative, risk-taking tone for your work that will stand you in good stead. Without valuing community building and developing relationships there will be no trust. Without trust, learning will be at best slow and at worst, shallow.

2   **Agree your values**. Spend time exploring the values and principles of the project at the start. Consider issues around how and what information will be shared as the project progresses and at the end. Think about any issues of confidentiality (you, your colleagues and your learners) the use of data, observation feedback, photographs, video and questions about e-safety (if you are using online sharing and research methods). Make sure you get the ethics of your project sorted right at the start so that you are all confident about 'working practices' as you begin your enquiries.

3   **Identify issues and areas of interest**. This needs to be both an individual and a group activity. Many action research models ask teachers to connect their line of enquiry to a specific school development priority. This is completely understandable. If a teacher is engaging in an enquiry programme of this kind, then it should, by the very nature of engagement, have a positive impact on the quality of students' learning experiences and connect with school priorities.

4   **Clarify your success criteria**. Know what you hope to achieve as a result of the time you are going to invest in this enquiry. Make sure the word 'learning' (both 'pupils learning' and 'my learning') appears in your success criteria as often as possible. Make sure you refine your criteria with at least one other person. For maximum impact, you could involve learners in your enquiry and see what they think. It may well be that you set up a parallel project where they enquire with you; this could form part of your evidence gathering from the outset. What if your learning buddy (see below) was a 13-year-old student? Or you were the learning buddy of a 15-year-old enquirer? Just a thought ...

5   **Identify what you *already* know about this**. It is highly unlikely that you will be undertaking an enquiry about which you know absolutely nothing or that you have never come across before. If it comes from issues and areas of personal interest, the chances are that you will already have given it some thought. In addition, you may have come across somebody else who has developed work in this area. It is at this point that you can start to identify how you might work with them.

Actively collaborate. Following on from (3), it is vital that you undertake your research with the help and support of others. This might be by finding a learning buddy. In this way, you can have someone to share your thoughts and findings with and they can act as a critical friend. You may ask them to observe you teaching when you are trying out new approaches or it may simply be a case of knowing that you have a regular and objective point of contact who can keep you on track when necessary and provide you with an audience for your successes (and 'failures'). It need not be another teacher and you may well decide between you that it will not be a reciprocal arrangement. If you are a member of a formally established enquiry group, there's scope for you to find a learning buddy beyond the immediate group. In this way, the group's connections and relationships will be enhanced by a greater sharing of knowledge between you all. This is particularly powerful in guarding against the silo-effect often experienced in these projects, where the learning and energy builds within a group of enthusiasts but fails to infect anyone beyond. This can be particularly counter-productive in terms of whole-school capacity building, as what was first a little hive of energy becomes an elite and exclusive group of innovators perceived by those who are not members as inaccessible and 'nothing to do with me'. One way to avoid this is to construct a whole-school professional development programme using action research or enquiry groups as the vehicle to promote a school-wide learning community. The trick is to maintain the focus on individual professional learning and its impact on the quality of learning as the *raison d'être* of the programme.

Any action research models should be flexible enough to meet two aims:

a   To foster 'bottom-up' innovation that develops a whole-school culture and ethos of learning.

b   To provide an opportunity for teachers to become learners. They can select their enquiry focus, design their own research methodology and use this learning to progress their own thinking and practice.

Share-as-you-go. Consider how you will share and reflect on your progress as the project unfolds. This is where you might leap into the digital world and set up a blog. You can document your thoughts, actions and observations as you go along. You can also identify key points on your timeline when you will critically reflect on what you have achieved along the way. Doing this online provides you with a public space where others can offer support and feedback. It is also a handy way to make sure that you draw on existing expertise as you go. A less onerous way of putting your ideas and thinking into the public domain could be to use Twitter. One tweet from your project in the form of a question has the potential of reaching thousands of educators from all over the world. That's some sharing-system. You are far more likely to follow up links and conduct online research if you're building up your own digital confidence through blogging and tweeting. In school, you could use a noticeboard in the staff room, a question box to share ideas and thinking from those not directly involved to answer questions from the group. Staff briefings are a handy way to give a two minute update on what your group is looking into, and ask others to get involved.

8. **Set your timeline.** Don't think that just because it's research it has to be long. Short bursts of enquiry are often just as powerful. Micro-enquiries that focus on one or two learners in a small part of a particular lesson are really useful to get into thinking reflectively. Just note down what you notice first. Then discuss with a partner what that might mean. This way, you can take the direction of your enquiry from what you know. Any theoretical knowledge you may have can then be aligned to that. Your next step can then be to extend your research. It may be that you select one term in which to develop work around independent learning. Within this, you might select three lessons with one group as the 'action' part of your research. Your enquiry, from identifying your focus to presenting your findings and agreeing upon your conclusion, could last no more than six weeks. Sorted. Leaving space for another. If your school is supportive of this model of individual professional development, it may be that you can agree some additional time to carry out your 'learning studies'. The beauty of this method is that you can start it all on your lonesome and carry out the research, reflection and collation of findings without it detracting from your other duties. To be honest, it could be argued that being reflective is an integral part of 'being curious', and as such, it is your 'duty'. This gives

you an opportunity to integrate your own learning into your teaching. We should be 'being' learners as often as we possibly can.

9 **Gather your evidence.** The only watchword is to be *creative*. Consider collecting evidence from different sources using a variety of methods. In addition to tried and tested methods, there are a heap of open-source (i.e. free!) online tools that can be used to engage others in your evidence collection. Even when it comes to observing a lesson, you can design the capture sheet according to what you actually want to look for, rather than just using a standard pro-forma. There is an example of a lesson observation capture sheet in Chapter 9 that is designed to capture types of questioning at different stages of the lesson. There's also an observation capture sheet specifically designed to record what types of activities are used at different stages of a lesson and another that focuses purely on how ideas and concepts are explained during the lesson (see pages 288 and 289). Interviews with learners are always incredibly valuable, so you might want to create some engaging ways to encourage authentic and less inhibited conversations such as setting up focus groups where you use card sorts or ranking exercises that are specific to the research you are doing. Think about who you ask to be involved in your focus groups to ensure you get a balanced view. There's nothing stopping you asking learners to co-design the way in which you find out their views or even ask them to act as research assistants on your behalf, if you think you'll get higher quality responses. Again, technology is a brilliant tool – by videoing or just recording the audio from learner conversations you will ensure you get verbatim comments that will offer you an honest insight into their views. You might also want to invite in an external visitor to ask questions of the students – this is where creativity with a learning buddy might come to the fore. What if your learning buddy came from another school? You could ask them to lead a student focus group and film or record their comments.

10 **Reflect, reflect, reflect.** Right the way through, take every opportunity to think deeply about your area of research. Have some self-evaluation questions as a script for your thinking:

How did doing this help me and my learners today?

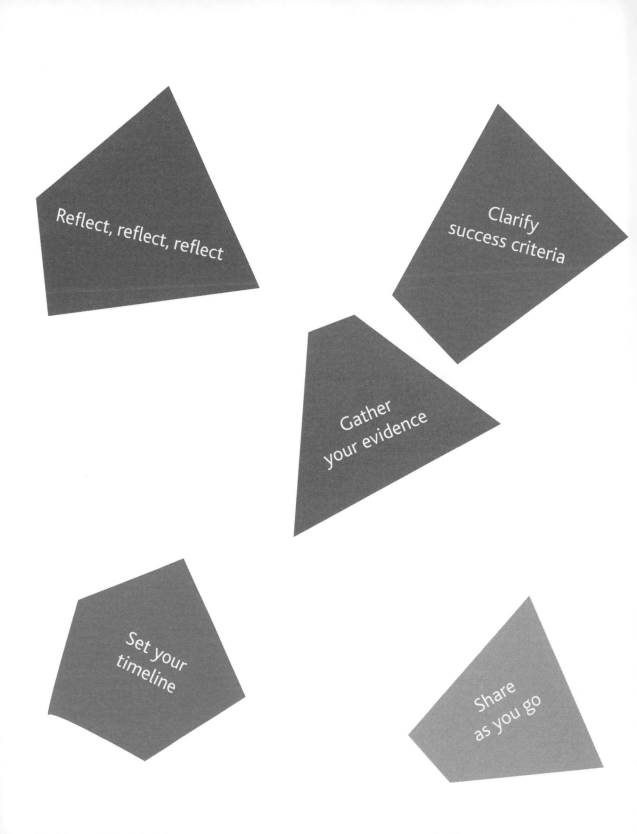

What change did I notice in the learning behaviours as a result of today's lesson?

What characteristics of effective group work did I see in Pupil A today?

How was this different to Pupil B?

How do I know Pupil C was learning, not just 'doing'?

What characteristics of quality learning conversations between Pupil D and Pupil E did I observe today?

How much did I talk in comparison with the students' talk?

How many quality questions did students generate today?

What was the balance of higher order questions from me/from students today?

Keep them visible and to hand. Tape them to your planner/desk. By keeping these questions at the forefront of your thinking, you'll also start constructing creative and imaginative ways to (a) capture the evidence of change, (b) deliberately offer targeted learning opportunities that will address the issues at the heart of your enquiry and (c) ask specific questions to assess progress and promote higher order thinking.

You can also share your reflective thinking with your class whenever you feel it is appropriate:

How did me doing this help you today?

Did you notice a difference in how we did this?

What do you think about learning in this way?

What's good/bad about organising the classroom like this?

11 **Share publicly .** Most definitions of what is meant by a powerful learning experience include the component of public affirmation. If learning happens in isolation, its power is limited to the one person who experienced it. Learning successes need to be shared, given life and celebrated. If we are to

model effective learning dispositions, develop intellectual and emotional resilience, receive praise and criticism and everything else that we seek to deliberately nurture in our students, we need to put our own heads above the parapet and learn what that feels like. After all, that's what we ask of all our learners on a regular basis. Sharing our research findings during a staff meeting or twilight session is one way of doing this. If we are blogging, then posting your final set of findings or observations, measured clearly against your stated success criteria, is another. Learning is social – every last ounce of it. Powerful learning is both personal and social (an interesting tension in itself).

Pupil activity observation sheet

TIME/EVENT LOG

(if used, this should be completed during the lesson)

Date:..Teacher:..

Sheet No:...

Lesson:...Observer:..

TIME	ACTIVITY CODE	DESCRIPTION OF ACTIVITES IN THE CLASSROOM

Suggested activity code:

1 = whole class work (interactive)

2 = whole class work (teacher led)

3 = individual work

4 = collaborative work

5 = classroom management

6 = testing/assessment

7 = transition between activities

8 = one-to-one support

Explaining observation sheet

Teacher		Subject	
Group		Observer(s)	
Lesson time		Date	

Clear structure Check current understanding Break down into distinct parts Sum up/recap	**Key ideas identified** Could be a central principle, generalisation, example or analogy	**Dynamic opening** A tease or hook to get pupils interested. Could be startling fact, or something not obviously connected	**Clarity** Vary the pitch, tone and volume of your voice. Body language is important, especially hands
Signposting Use emphasising phrases such as 'and the important thing is ... ' or 'there are three stages: first ... '	**Examples and non-examples** Useful to illustrate a point with an example, a non example helps pupils to build a more complex understanding	**Models and analogies** To be able to visualise objects that are too big or small, processes that can't be directly seen, abstract ideas	**Props** A picture or object is particularly helpful to visual learners
Questions Helps you to monitor pupils' understanding	**Connect to pupils' experience** Gives pupils a base on which to build new learning, and helps them to make links	**Repetition** Helps to emphasise a key point. Use much more in speech than you would in writing	**Humour** Helps keep pupils' attention

Teachers as 21st century learners

The active seeking out of ideas, strategies and resources to progress our professional learning is so much easier with the growth of the digital world. I have learnt so much from the quality learning conversations in which I have engaged over the past year on Twitter and through blogging.

But it's a strange thing, this digital world, or at least people's reaction to it. Sometimes it can feel a bit like trying to convince someone that they should take up a new sport or hobby because *you* really enjoy or, at its most extreme, that they should join you in a cult. The more evangelical you get about it, the more you tend to turn people away from it. The bottom line for me is that there really isn't a choice for us as educators as to whether we should or shouldn't get involved in the digital world. If we are going to prepare learners to make a positive contribution to the world, we need to help them be digitally literate. The only way to do that is for us to become digitally literate. The digital world, with its huge potential (for good and not-so-good) is a reality and it's not going away.

The emergence of the new technologies associated with Web 2.0 brings with it amazing opportunities for interaction and feedback. It is at this intersection of people, ideas, information, communication and skills – that change – learning – occurs.

Professional development and Web 2.0 – a brief why, how and what

The following list is a snapshot of just some of the reasons I have seen as to why educators are so excited about the opportunities Web 2.0 is offering them in their own professional development.

Why?

I want to connect with a worldwide group of educators from whom I can learn about teaching and learning in a variety of subject areas, cohorts of students, social backgrounds, global education systems and pedagogical approaches.

I want to access a diverse collection of resources created and quality assured by people whose opinions I trust and respect on the basis of what they have shared already through their previous recommendations and blogs.

I haven't got loads of time to trawl the web and find new resources. I need a fast and quality assured personalised search engine.

Sometimes I don't know what I'm looking for, so I need to have a deep pool of ideas to pick from and adapt. I need to be surprised by what others are doing that I haven't even thought about.

How?

I have a smartphone and a laptop that I can use for quick and easy access to the web. This means I can have a constant stream of ideas coming straight to me and I can put 10–15 minutes aside to check them out.

Once I have built up my confidence, I want to contribute to the stream of information and share some of my own ideas and finds. I need to be able to do this quickly and in a way and at a time that suits me.

When I am confident enough, I want to start blogging my personal learning reflections and get feedback to see what other people think about my work. I need to be able to let people know about my blog by sharing links with them and asking for their comments.

What?

 Twitter restricts entries to 140 characters, so every 'tweet' is simple and easy to either follow-up or pass over.

 I can access information from my computer, tablet or my phone, so whatever is more convenient for me, I will use.

 Twitter's use of themed conversations and searches (using what is called a hashtag i.e. the # sign) allows me to focus in on topic-specific resources.

I can build a personal learning community of educators to whom I can direct specific questions and with whom I can develop long-standing professional relationships and meet up with and visit at their schools.

Go build your boat!

A colleague said to me recently, 'There's nothing new in education, only ideas (some good and some not so) that get recycled'. It's a common refrain but, on reflection, not one I totally agree with. If anything, the last few years have taught me that even though the themes may seem familiar, there is one significant difference in our fast developing environment.

It's us.

And it's them.

We're all new and we all bring that newness to every learning opportunity that we design. Nothing happens in a vacuum and those learners in front of us weren't there twenty years ago when we may have first talked about Bloom's Taxonomy, the importance of creativity or the first flourishes of The National Curriculum. They are here now and they are very different from those learners two decades ago.

They have new and more challenging expectations. They expect to be involved and asked for their views. They expect to be engaged by interesting and exciting ideas, meaningfully presented. They are used to myriad sources of information which they filter fast and discard even quicker.

But they also need our help because, for all their bluster, the world can seem a scary place where the certainties of old no longer exist. They must be resilient, reflexive and adaptive. They must be resourceful and creative. These are the qualities required of all of them in their new world with its exhausting challenges and opportunities. And these are the qualities they have within them, just waiting to be drawn out.

You are new too, just as influenced by new technologies and thinking, by new ways of working and by the learners themselves. You are interested in ideas from outside your field and how you can incorporate them with your own.

And that's what Full On Learning is about. Learning is complex. There's a lot to it. So try stuff out and see what works. When it does, make sure you know why. And when it doesn't, make sure you know why. Don't think you have to throw it all in, all the time. Have big conversations, yes, but take baby steps. Get used to the principles, let your ideas flow from what you've read here into what you already know, do and are like as a practitioner.

The river awaits.

Lucy Sweetman

Black, P. and Wiliam, D., *Inside the Black Box: Raising Standards through Classroom Assessment* (London: King's College, 1988).

Chatfield, T., *Fun Inc.: Why Games are the 21st Century's Most Serious Business* (London: Virgin Books, 2010).

Coyle, D., *The Talent Code: Greatness Isn't Born. It's Grown. Here's How* (New York: Bantam, 2009).

Curran, A., *The Little Book of Big Stuff About the Brain* (Carmarthen: Crown House Publishing, 2008).

de Bono, E., *Six Thinking Hats: An Essential Approach to Business Management* (Boston, MA: Little, Brown and Company, 1985).

Diamond, J., *Guns, Germs and Steel: A Short History of Everybody for the Last 13,000 Years* (London: Vintage, 1998).

Douglas, T. and Seely Brown, J., *A New Culture of Learning: Cultivating the Imagination for a World of Constant Change* (CreateSpace, 2011).

Dweck, C. S., *Mindset: The New Psychology of Success* (New York: Random House, 2006).

Ericsson, K. A., Prietula, M. J. and Cokely, E. T., The Making of an Expert. *Harvard Business Review* 85 (7/8) (2007): 114–121. Available at http://www.coachingmanagement.nl/The%20 Making%20of%20an%20Expert.pdf (accessed 11 October 2011).

Friedman, T. L., *The World Is Flat: A Brief History of the Twenty-First Century*, updated and expanded (New York: Farrar, Straus and Giroux, 2006).

Gallo, C., *The Innovation Secrets of Steve Jobs: Insanely Different Principles for Breakthrough Success* (Columbus, OH: McGraw-Hill, 2010).

Gilbert, C. (chair), *2020 Vision: Report of the Teaching and Learning in 2020 Review Group* (Nottingham: DfES, 2007).

Giles, N. and Hayman, M., *Disruptive Influence: The Entrepreneur Report from Virgin Media Pioneers* (2010). Available at http://www.virginmediapioneers.com/files/2010/09/Disruptive-Influence-The-Entrepreneur-Report.pdf (accessed 11 October 2011).

Gladwell, M., *Blink: The Power of Thinking without Thinking* (New York: Little, Brown and Company, 2005).

Gladwell, M., *Outliers: The Story of Success* (New York: Little, Brown and Company, 2008).

Hattie, J., *Visible Learning* (Abingdon: Routledge, 2009).

Kahneman, D., *Thinking, Fast and Slow*, (London: Penguin, 2011).

BIBLIOGRAPHY

Kelling, G. L. and Coles, C., *Fixing Broken Windows: Restoring Order and Reducing Crime in Our Communities* (New York: Simon & Schuster, 1998).

Leadbeater, C., *We-Think: Mass Innovation, Not Mass Production* (London: Profile Books, 2008).

National Advisory Committee on Creative and Cultural Education, *All Our Futures: Creativity, Culture and Education* (London: NACCCE, 1999). Available at http://www.cypni.org.uk/downloads/alloutfutures.pdf (accessed 11 October 2011).

Pink, D., *A Whole New Mind: Why Right-Brainers Will Rule the Future* (New York: Marshall Cavendish, 2008).

Pink, D. *Drive: The Surprising Truth About What Motivates Us* Pink (Edinburgh: Canongate Books Ltd, 2010).

Pinker, S., *The Language Instinct: How the Mind Creates Meaning* (New York: Harper Perennial Modern Classics, 2000).

Qualifications and Curriculum Authority, *Cross-Curriculum Dimensions: A Planning Guide for Schools* (London: QCA, 2009). Available at http://curriculum.qcda.gov.uk/uploads/Cross%20curriculum%20dimensions%20-%20a%20planning%20guide%20for%20schools%20publication_tcm8-14464.pdf (accessed 11 October 2011).

Renzulli, J. S., The Three-Ring Conception of Giftedness: A Developmental Model for Promoting Creative Productivity. In R. J. Sternberg and J. E. Davidson (eds), *Conceptions of Giftedness* (Cambridge: Cambridge University Press, 2005), pp. 53–92. Available at http://www.gifted.uconn.edu/sem/pdf/The_Three-Ring_Conception_of_Giftedness.pdf (accessed 11 October 2011).

Renzulli, J. S. and Reis, S. M., *The Schoolwide Enrichment Model*, 2nd edn (Mansfield Center, CT: Creative Learning Press, 1997).

Sinek, S., *Start with Why: How Great Leaders Inspire Everyone to Take Action* (London: Penguin, 2011).

Shirky, C., *Cognitive Surplus: Creativity and Generosity in a Connected Age* (London: Penguin, 2010)

Smith, J., *The Lazy Teacher's Handbook* (Carmarthen: Crown House Publishing, 2010).

Wesch, M., From Knowledgeable to Knowledge-able: Experiments in New Media Literacy. Keynote speech, ELI Annual Conference, Orlando, Florida, 21 January 2009. Available at http://www.academiccommons.org/commons/essay/knowledgable-knowledge-able (accessed 11 October 2011).

INDEX

Q

R

S

Zoë Elder's book makes a compelling case for teachers' and students' effortful engagement in the many processes of learning, and she sure walks the talk: this book exudes hundreds of hours of thought, reflection, planning, redrafting and reorganising, and it's all the better for it. The author clearly has a relentless curiosity (more talk-walking), and a remarkable capacity to synthesise wide reading at the frontiers of educational theory in a format which is attractive, accessible and very readable - without once talking down to her reader. On the contrary, potential readers of this valuable addition to the canon of classroom praxis had better be prepared to step up. If they do, they will find much to intrigue, provoke and feed their appetite for educational excellence, and they will take away practical strategies for translating often subtle insights into the rich melee of the classroom.

Barry J Hymer. Professor of Psychology in Education, University of Cumbria

Full On Learning sits at that intersection where the craft of teaching meets the science of learning. Packed with practical ideas, it proves what Zoë expounds: that effective teaching is fundamentally a creative activity which focuses relentlessly on teasing out the capacity and potential of each student. Defining an architecture, creating with the building blocks, it will not only transform classrooms but also take teaching and learning experiences to another level.

Sir John Jones. Writer, presenter, educational consultant

Full On Learning will inspire school leaders, energise class teachers, provide essential wisdom to politicians and may just recharge those in the profession who have lost their way.

This is a 'done with' not a 'done to' resource. If you're after a series of photocopiable lesson plans, look elsewhere; if you want a guru to make all your classroom challenges go away, it's the next shelf down. But if you are a head teacher seeking inspiration to lead, or a class teacher wanting processes to make learning more relevant, then read on.

Zoë sets her expectations high. She assumes you to want to prepare your pupils for their 21st century digital futures, not some long-gone mythical golden age; she believes in you as a professional learner and proficient classroom researcher and she offers you a design process for seizing back your passion and your creativity.

Each of the 12 sections explores an indispensable feature of successful learning, using well-honed text and visuals that support meaning rather than invade it. The book is scattered with genuine action research prompts that engage and challenge classroom practice: 'What is a risk for me in my own practice' or 'How do I establish a safe learning community for all learners?' are typical nudges to get us thinking about learning.

Zoë's standards are high, but they are broad standards of human learning, not restrictive measures of pupil achievement. To apply the book's opening metaphor, 'Full On Learning' is not the hired boat that will take you over one river but the principles, skills, confidence and motivation to build your own and to sail it anywhere.

Mike Fleetham. Learning Designer, www.thinkingclassroom.co.uk

All teachers need hope, and the infectious enthusiasm and expert advice that Zoë Elder gives in *Full On Learning* is just the medicine needed to believe that we can make a difference in our schools.

If you are feeling under pressure from the relentless nature of school life, then this beautifully presented book will help you remember that it is what you do in your classroom which truly affects the children and young people you work with.

You may have implemented the best of the National Strategies in your primary school and Zoë's book will provide you with the next set of ideas to move your teaching and your colleagues to good and beyond. In a secondary school you may be grappling with impact of The Wolf Report and recognise that the route to progress is less likely to be through curriculum changes, so instead the road map for improving classroom interactions given in *Full On Learning* is perfectly timed.

If you are truly trying to develop 'Outstanding' teaching and learning in your class-room, your department, your Key Stage or in your school, then you must read Zoë Elder's *Full On Learning*.

Paul Ainsworth, Acting Principal and author of *Get that Teaching Job*

Full on Learning is a book that is so inviting that it forces you to turn the pages.

Zoë is steeped in teaching and learning. Reflection, synthesis and practical tips ooze from every 'full on' chapter. It is a wonderful *tour-de-force* that needs to be in the library of every teacher and required reading on ITT courses. From the example of a 3-year-old who can happily use apps on an iPhone, to the power of outcome-based planning and collaborative learning for all ages, Zoë shows that learning is at a step-change. We have to embrace digital technology and we have to see teaching as an apposite, but crucial, interruption to learning. With *Full On Learning* and Zoë Elder we have a new force in educational thinking.

Paul Garvey. Educational consultant and owner of QA South-West.

Full On Learning is a 'must have' book for any professional learning facilitator. Zoë articulates principles for learning, in a simple, accessible way, which are deeply consistent with what we now know from research about deep learning and quality student engagement. This is a radical 21st century approach to teaching as learning design, something that is going to become a core professional competence for teachers and learning and development specialists in the information age. Each chapter takes a profound idea – involvement, creativity, entrepreneurial learning, collaboration, feedback, motivation, questioning – and presents it simply, including both the why and the how. This book is an essential text for any teacher who is passionate about deep learning.

Ruth Deakin Crick. Reader in Systems Learning and Leadership,
Graduate School of Education, University of Bristol

Zoë's book really does provide a must-have read, 'a blueprint for teachers', for the 21st Century and beyond. It is invaluable for all educators, from the NQT to the nearly-retired; after all, as the author states, 'Learning is far too important to be left to chance'.

Because 'everything a teacher does and says in the classroom counts', *Full On Learning* helps us know, understand and learn about how to improve our practice to instigate the best possible learning opportunities for the young people in our care; learning that will help them now, and in a fast-changing and very uncertain future.

This book, 'truly involves the reader in the learning' and emphasises the importance of planning and preparation, as well as the need for effective questioning and well-honed feedback. As such, Zoë helps us to explore the why, what, when and how to create successful learners, and therefore life-long learners, equipped to respond to a range of new situations and unforeseen predicaments.

I particularly like the Action Research questions which help the reader focus on how to bring to practice the ideas and themes explored in each of the chapters. These are perfect for developing self-reflecting practice and developing our own ideas towards how they can encompass and develop our very own Full On Learning experiences … look out for the green boxes!

Finally, and of invaluable use to anyone in the challenging world of teaching, is the advice, suggestions and prompts that Zoë gives us on risk taking, emotional awareness, creative thinking and thinking cultures – all in the name of creating powerful learners. Combine this with her tremendous insights into questioning and motivation and you have a wealth of techniques to create the learning entrepreneurs that we need for a successful society of tomorrow.

If you believe we all 'have a duty to be curious', I urge you to buy this book, to 'build your boat' and make a difference in your classrooms.

Suzie Levett. School Improvement Adviser

This very special book is a beautifully produced treatise on learning. Each page is a pleasure, with something new to learn and explore. It reminds me of when I first got my iPad: it was so full of interesting things I took it everywhere and played with it endlessly, constantly surprising myself with its potential. The same with Zoë's book - there is so much in it that I know it will be filled with Post-it notes and bookmarks on every teacher's bookshelf.

This book really does cover everything you need to know about learning for the 21st century. The author's voice is consistently heard throughout the book, demanding that we consider the importance of the learners owning their experiences and being fully engaged to reach their amazing potential. This book also practises what it preaches, as it is fun and engaging and makes you think in different ways. It also sets up very useful checklists and informative links to make it an extremely practical read too.

I haven't read a better book that sums up all the essentials for outstanding learning in such an engaging format that will make it one of my most treasured tomes, lovingly taken everywhere and only lent to trusted friends.

Teacher, buy this book!

Jackie Beere OBE, author, trainer and educationalist